June 2023 ·······················

TZU CHI GLOBAL
REFUGEE RELIEF
EXHIBITION

UPROOTED:
Compassion After Displacement

Edited by Tzu Chi Center
&
Tzu Chi Culture and Communications Department

BUDDHIST TZU CHI FOUNDATION

May 2024, Tzu Chi Center, New York

Title:	UPROOTED: Compassion After Displacement – Tzu Chi Global Refugee Relief Exhibition
Producer:	Kate Chao (Director of Tzu Chi Center)
Production Director:	Freeman Su (Executive Director of Buddhist Tzu Chi Foundation, Northeast Region)
Project Executive:	Zi Ye
Production Manager:	Annie Chu, Yinhsu Liu
Designer:	Zi Ye, Catherine Lee, Ling Soo
Cover Design:	Peng-San Mok, Beng-Lan Seow
Exhibition Design:	Culture and Communications Department, Tzu Chi USA
Chief Editor:	Zi Ye, Yu-Yi Shen
Art Editor:	PUSAMAM DIGITAL CULTURE CO., LTD.
Text Editor:	Limei Xu, Xuehui Tang, Ariel Tsai, Qihua Luo, Zi Ye, Pheel Wang, Hon-Chan Lin
Translator:	Yinhsu Liu, Ariel Tsai, Joy Chang, William James Spencer, Zi Ye
Editor and Proofreader (Chinese):	Shu-Yi Chiang, Ching-Hsin Yang, Susan Chou
Editor and Proofreader (English):	Rosalie Chen, Yinhsu Liu, Chloe Chan
Sources:	Tzu Chi Media Database, Tzu Chi Global Website, Tzu Chi Monthly, Tzu Chi USA Journal, TCNews
Trade publisher:	Sbooker Publications, a division of Cite Publishing Ltd.
Publisher:	Ho, Fei-Peng
Editor-in-chief:	Chia, Chun-Kuo
Address:	8F., No.141, Sec.2 Minsheng E. Rd.,Taipei,Taiwan
Tel. number:	02-25007008
Publication date:	Mar. 2024
ISBN:	978-626-7431-21-4
EISBN:	978-626-7431-22-1(EPUB)

Library of Congress Cataloging-in-Publication Data has been applied for.

======

The "UPROOTED: Compassion After Displacement" exhibition and publication of this commemorative book represents only a small part in the vast public discourse on global refugees relief efforts. However small it may be, may our actions trigger broader ripples of love and kindness. Thank you to everyone who has contributed to this cause.

— Tzu Chi Center

PREVIOUS PAGE: Tzu Chi and Knightsbridge International (KBI) of the United States provide relief in Afghanistan. In addition to material assistance, they also instilled hope for the future in those who were suffering. Photo: Zhihong Wang

After joint forces led by the United States and United Kingdom sent troops to invade Iraq, Tzu Chi volunteers reached out to care for Iraqi refugees who fled to Jordan. Jordan Tzu Chi volunteer, Chiou-hwa Chen, blows balloons and interacts with refugee children. Photo: Junfu Wang

Contents

UPROOTED: the Exhibition

Tzu Chi Center

Colors from El Menahil

Tzu Chi Refugee Relief Timeline

Love is Hope

Love is the energy that will
sustain peace in this world.

—Jing Si Aphorism by Master Cheng Yen

Preface

PO-WEN YEN

CEO of Buddhist Tzu Chi Charity Foundation

First of all, I would like to express my gratitude to the Tzu Chi team from the United States for their dedicated efforts in organizing the exhibition, "UPROOTED: Compassion After Displacement," held at the Tzu Chi Center for Compassionate Relief in New York. I sincerely congratulate you on the publication of this memorial book, making the important contributions of this exhibition available for the future.

Around the world, the COVID-19 pandemic has further impoverished the poor, and the outbreak of the Russia-Ukraine war has not only exacerbated global inflation, food, and energy crises, but has also pushed the total number of forcibly displaced people beyond 100 million. At the onset of the conflict, Tzu Chi volunteers from twelve countries, under the compassionate guidance of Dharma Master Cheng Yen, gathered in Poland to assist Ukrainian refugees. Through collaboration with eleven international and national NGOs, Tzu Chi's humanitarian aid has reached Ukraine as well as refugees in eight neighboring countries.

The assistance given includes shopping cards, cash cards, cold weather supplies, healthcare services, medicine, language and children's education, psychological and legal counseling, and financial support to individuals and families. This assistance has been uninterrupted and continues even now. Moreover, some of our volunteers who were themselves refugees in Poland have returned to Ukraine and are determined to bring Tzu Chi's aid and humanitarian care back to their homeland.

In Türkiye, Tzu Chi volunteers Faisal Hu, Nadya Chou and David Yu have established a solid foundation for assisting Syrian refugees. In 2015, they initiated and helped Tzu Chi found the El Menahil International School, providing education opportunities for Syrian refugee children who were working in factories. Eight years later, many of these young Syrians became Tzu Chi volunteers themselves after the major earthquake in 2023. These youths developed and improved an online system to handle the extensive data of disaster victims.

From registration, notifications, identity verification to distribution, this system has enabled Tzu Chi to provide rapid and smooth assistance to earthquake survivors. This truly represents a cycle of kindness.

When I traveled to Türkiye in July, 2023, I witnessed the partnership of great compassion between Tzu Chi Foundation and the Muslim population in Istanbul. Together, we are providing education and hope to the children of Syrian refugees in Türkiye. I hope that the construction of the new campus of Tzu Chi's El Menahil International School can be quickly completed so the school can improve the lives of even more students.

Similarly, in Malaysia, Thailand, and the United States, Tzu Chi volunteers show care for local refugees without distinctions of nationality, political views, or religion. With selfless love and fearlessness in the face of adversity, they reach out to refugees to assist them in rebuilding their education and livelihoods.

Finally, I would like to emphasize how, in the past few years, geopolitical tensions and power struggles between countries have made the global situation increasingly precarious. Master Cheng Yen often prays for "all people's hearts to be purified, for all societies to be in harmony, and for the world to be free of disasters." The key to all of this is people's hearts and minds. We hope that this book will help more people understand that it is only through the awakening of humanity to mutual assistance, mutual love, and shared goodness that we can achieve harmony in the world, sustainability of the earth, and a promising future for humanity.

Post-disaster Follow-Up Visit in Türkiye, 2023
On July 16, Po-Wen Yen, CEO of Tzu Chi Charity Foundation, led a team to Türkiye for progress review. The team first went to Gaziantep Province, the earthquake-stricken region, to learn about the direction of the government's follow-up reconstruction. Photo: Lichen Chou

BELOW: Internally displaced children in Kelly, town of Syria's Idlib Governorate, found new ways to play in this war and earthquake-torn region of the country. Photo: courtesy of Bakr Al Kasem for Doctors of the World Türkiye

FOLLOWING PAGES: Women and children in Kelly located in northwestern Syria's Idlib are waiting for a consultation at Kelly Clinic, operated in cooperation with Doctors of the World Türkiye and Tzu Chi Foundation as the sole medical center responding to the health needs of people in the region. Photo: courtesy of Bakr Al Kasem for Doctors of the World Türkiye

Striving for Peace

All faiths believe in kindness.
With a shared goal of love,
naturally we'll work united toward global peace.

—Jing Si Aphorism by Master Cheng Yen

GLOBAL

PARTNERS

Unveiling the Power of Unity:

A Deep Dive into Global Alliances, Interfaith Cooperation, and Tzu Chi Foundation's Role in Disaster Management

BRANDA NG

Director of Tzu Chi Global Partnership Affairs Department

The world is facing an increasing frequency of catastrophic events, which emphasizes the importance of global partnerships with faith-based organizations. These entities can mobilize aid quickly and effectively due to their extensive networks and resources. One such organization that stands out in disaster management is the Buddhist Tzu Chi Charity Foundation, which highlights the significance of interfaith collaborations in its relief operations.

Rooted in Buddhist teachings, Tzu Chi Foundation showcases how faith-based entities can make a significant contribution to relief work. They offer both material aid and emotional and spiritual comfort to those affected. Tzu Chi's commitment to interfaith cooperation is a distinguishing feature of its methodology. By acknowledging the universal principles shared among various religions, Tzu Chi actively seeks partnerships with organizations of diverse faiths.

This interfaith collaboration allows for a wider reach and a more diverse array of resources during crises. Tzu Chi's disaster response initiatives, particularly its interfaith collaborations, highlight the potential of faith-based entities in global alliances. Their efforts underscore the necessity of incorporating these organizations into broader disaster response strategies, recognizing their unique abilities and contributions.

On April 30 2022, the Buddhist Tzu Chi Charity Foundation and the Camillian Disaster Service International (CADIS) signed a memorandum of understanding (MOU) to expand the assistance to the Ukrainian refugees. The joint effort in Poland and Ukraine includes the distribution of food and daily necessities, cash cards, medical services, resettlement shelters, psychological counseling, skills training, and other humanitarian assistance. Video conference participants from Taiwan, Poland, and Rome, Italy joined online to witness the signing ceremony. Photo: Tzu Chi Foundation

On April 2022, the Buddhist Tzu Chi Charity Foundation and the Camillian Disaster Service International (CADIS) signed a commitment to operate jointly in Poland and Ukraine to extend aid to Ukrainian refugees. The aid included the provision of daily necessities, food, medical services, temporary housing, and psychological counseling to help more than 40,000 people over a period of about five months. During the signing ceremony, CADIS representatives and Dharma Masters from the Jing Si Abode (Tzu Chi headquarter) led the participants during the video conference from Taiwan, Poland, and Rome to pray together for the war to end and for the world to be free of disasters.

Tzu Chi's aid, including daily necessities, food, medical services, temporary housing, and psychological counseling, is vital in assisting individuals and families to reconstruct their lives after experiencing the devastating effects of war and displacement. Providing medical supplies to healthcare facilities in Ukraine and communities hosting refugees in the Republic of Moldova is crucial in addressing the immediate health needs of those affected by the conflict.

In May 2022, Tzu Chi committed $10 million to UNICEF's emergency response to support vulnerable children and families affected by the ongoing war in Ukraine. This is just one instance of the remarkable work Tzu Chi is doing to positively impact the lives of those in need.

The support from Tzu Chi Foundation will help UNICEF provide critical protection services for children and families, including the identification of unaccompanied children, psychosocial support, and protection from sexual exploitation and abuse, among others. In addition to supporting UNICEF, Tzu Chi Foundation has also provided physical goods alongside much needed psychosocial and emotional spiritual care to refugee families across three cities in Poland.

By ensuring access to medical services and supplies, Tzu Chi and consortium are helping to alleviate suffering and improve the overall well-being of those in need. The partnership between Tzu Chi Foundation and the consortium of NGOs, including Airlink, ADRA International, Project HOPE, and World Hope International, is a shining example of the impact of organizations working collaboratively towards a common goal.

At the Memorandum of Understanding, or MOU, signing ceremony on June 2, 2022, Airlink President and CEO Steven J. Smith explained, "Responding meaningfully to human suffering on this scale requires a coordinated effort from multiple sectors, public, private, and philanthropic, utilizing the skills, expertise, and resources of each to bring aid and hope to the people of Ukraine. I'm absolutely delighted that Airlink, along with partners ADRA, Project HOPE, World Hope International, and the Buddhist Tzu Chi Charity Foundation will work together in this important consortium to address these humanitarian needs."

Buddhist Tzu Chi Charity Foundation CEO

Mr. Po-Wen Yen added, "In recognizing that this crisis requires collaborative efforts to ensure that all needs are met with compassion, gratitude, respect, and love, Tzu Chi is excited to partner with Airlink, ADRA, Project HOPE, and World Hope International to provide necessities and medical items to displaced Ukrainians."

By working together, Tzu Chi and consortium of NGOs can maximize their collective efforts to provide much-needed aid and support to vulnerable populations affected by the conflict in Ukraine. Their commitment to positively impacting the lives of those in need is commendable and inspiring. As we continue to face numerous global challenges, partnerships such as these give us hope for a better and more compassionate world.

LEFT: Children play in a Spilno Child Spot in Odesa, Ukraine, which serves as a platform for integrated psycho-social support, health, and education services for children and their families. The war is impacting millions of children's education, development, and other basic needs. UNICEF has created over 150 child-friendly Spilno Hubs across Ukraine. Photo: courtesy of UNICEF

Doctors of the World Türkiye, Medical Station in Idlib Governorate, Syria

Tzu Chi Foundation signed a charity cooperation with the Doctors of the World Türkiye to provide medical assistance to the earthquake victims in Syria. Between April to August 2023, they served 13,117 people. The square iron rooftop house in the center of the picture is the medical station of the Doctors of the World Türkiye, the only medical facility in the region. It serves 23 nearby refugee camps, benefiting 55,000 people. Photo: courtesy of Doctors of the World

"Children and families in Ukraine have had their lives uprooted for more than a year while enduring violence, trauma, destruction and displacement. With the support of partners like the Buddhist Tzu Chi Foundation, UNICEF can continue to provide lifesaving assistance to those affected by the ongoing war."

MICHAEL J. NYENHUIS

President and Chief Executive Officer, UNICEF USA

"Tzu Chi has been an incredible partner for IsraAID. I met Tzu Chi in many disaster areas around the world, and right now, we're collaborating in Ukraine, Moldova, and Romania to provide both immediate relief with their supplies, [and] psycho-social support to hundreds of thousands of people."

YOTAM POLIZER

Chief Executive Officer, IsraAID

"It's hard to understate the scale of this crisis, but it's not just the scale, but the speed with which it developed. And that put a tremendous burden on the Ukrainian health system... [and] frontline healthcare workers, which is what Project HOPE exists to do as its mission, is support frontline healthcare workers around the world. This consortium is here to do some extremely important, critical, time sensitive work."

CHRIS SKOPEC

Executive Vice President, Project HOPE

"Buddha's mercy and God's love exist to save people who suffer, and our fundamental values are the same. We must face and cooperate for the sake of Ukrainians who are experiencing difficulties. Ours is a great responsibility, as well as a mission, and we want to offer respect and assistance to Ukrainian refugees with gratitude and love."

BR. JOSÉ IGNACIO SANTAOLALLA SAEZ
President, Camillian Disaster Service International

"In life, we see these forces constantly pulling us apart, but in times of disaster, we find these common existential threats that bring us together. And that gives me hope for humanity that people like us can come together [and find] a larger solution than any one of us could solve on our own."

JOHN LYON
President and Chief Executive Officer, World Hope International

"By working in a consortium, we come together to deliver to our partners the resources and capacity so we can together impact more. Usually in a situation, in an emergency, we address the immediate needs, the life-saving needs of food, water, shelter, and sometimes, we neglect, due to resources, and the complexity of logistics, the need for medical supplies. So, in this case we really appreciate this partnership, because it is much needed."

IMAD MADANAT
Vice President for Programs, Adventist Development and Relief Agency

Relief for Ukrainian Refugees in Opole, Poland, 2022

Tzu Chi cooperated with an entrepreneur couple and the government in Opole, Poland to distribute cash cards to Ukrainian refugees at the Opole Stegu Arena from July 26 to 29. Refugees entered the site to receive aid. Photo: Shu Wei Chen

The Power of Partnership:
Airlink and Tzu Chi Foundation

STEVEN J. SMITH

President and CEO of Airlink

The Buddhist Tzu Chi Charity Foundation has been, and remains, an invaluable partner to Airlink. Working together over the last two years, we have made a significant difference in the lives of thousands of people impacted by natural disasters and other humanitarian crises. As the President and CEO of Airlink, I feel tremendously grateful to have the support of Tzu Chi, your leadership, and your dedicated staff and volunteers.

Airlink's mission is to help communities impacted by disasters and other humanitarian crises. We do this by providing non-governmental organizations (NGOs) with free air transport for their expert responders and humanitarian supplies. We believe transport costs and other logistic challenges should not hinder NGO partners from responding to crises and ensuring life-sustaining help reaches the world's most vulnerable people. We are grateful Tzu Chi shares this belief and partners with Airlink to address humanitarian needs.

The role of logistics in bringing help to people and communities recovering from crisis is often unrecognized. On average, supply chain management accounts for 73% of the cost of any humanitarian program, with transport being one of the process's most costly and cost-volatile components. Tzu Chi's understanding of and support for the critical role of logistics in humanitarian response has been extremely important to our efforts to deliver aid.

In the spring of 2022, Airlink launched our largest humanitarian response to support communities affected by the war in Ukraine. Thanks to outstanding support from Tzu Chi, Airlink leveraged the capabilities of reputable and experienced NGO partners to bring life-saving medical supplies, hygiene items, and durable medical equipment to Ukrainians trapped in the conflict and refugees seeking safety in Moldova, Poland, Hungary, Slovakia, and Romania. As a result, more than 70 medical centers were provided with health care supplies and medicines, mobile medical units offered primary health care to those cut off from help in eastern Ukraine, and communities received food and other essential items. Nearly half

Aid Operation for Ukrainian Refugees in Romania, 2022

After Poland, Romania is currently the second-largest host country for Ukrainian refugees. In a joint effort involving IsraAID, other international NGOs, local Ukrainian humanitarian aid groups, and Tzu Chi, a humanitarian relief logistics center was established in Turda, Romania, dedicated to aiding Ukrain. In May, Tzu Chi's United Nations team visited the site to understand its operational procedures and to identify the urgent types of medical supplies needed. Photo: Tzu Chi USA

a million people were helped through the partnership.

Airlink has also enjoyed supporting Tzu Chi's relief efforts by donating more than $480,000 in transportation and logistics services to the organization, enabling their work in response to the war in Ukraine and flooding in Pakistan.

The difference partnership makes to the sustainability of aid operations, and ultimately the positive impact on communities in need, should not be underestimated. Airlink's partnership with Tzu Chi has enabled assistance to many communities and enabled recovery support to be sustained.

We sincerely thank Tzu Chi Foundation for your support and partnership, and we look forward to strengthening our collaboration in 2023 and beyond.

Tzu Chi Foundation signed a MOU with four international organizations for humanitarian assistance to care for Ukrainian refugees, 2022

As the Russia-Ukraine war persists, Tzu Chi continues to work with international NGOs and interfaith organizations. On June 2, a memorandum of understanding (MOU) was signed online, with CEO Po-Wen Yen (right) representing Tzu Chi Foundation, along with four NGOs: Airlink, Adventist Development and Relief Agency (ADRA), Project Hope, and World Hope International. The collaboration aims to transport a greater amount of urgently needed medicine, medical equipment, and other essential supplies to Ukrainian refugees. Pictured left is Vice CEO Chang Tsung-yi of Tzu Chi Foundation. Photo: Yi-Chien Chen

Airlink and the Buddhist Tzu Chi Charity Foundation in Action:

Through Airlink's network-based model of partnership and cooperation, Airlink helps provide a greater degree of aid coordination, reducing waste and duplication in a fragmented sector. Tzu Chi Foundation was key in one of Airlink's most significant contributions to delivering aid to Ukrainians caught in the war.

Moldova and Ukraine:

With a grant of $3 million from the Buddhist Tzu Chi Charity Foundation, Airlink led and coordinated a consortium of NGOs and funding to reach Ukrainians needing healthcare and other critical assistance across Ukraine, Poland, Hungary, Moldova, Romania, and Slovakia. Of particular concern was supplying medical assistance to Ukrainians in Moldova, which at the time had the highest per capita number of refugees than any other country. Despite the generosity of the people of Moldova, this was placing a huge strain on the health care system of the country, pushing it to near breaking point.

Through partnership, Airlink NGO partners and consortium members ADRA, Project HOPE, and World Hope International provided vital aid to clinics treating Ukrainian refugees. This project, completed in December 2022, was focused on three goals:

1. Delivering critically needed medicines, medical equipment, and supplies to treat conflict-related trauma and provide health care related to chronic illnesses, primary care, and infectious diseases.

2. Strengthening overburdened and under-resourced health systems in Ukraine and Moldova.

3. Removing transportation and logistics barriers to increase the amount of aid available to support those sheltering in place, internally displaced people in Ukraine, and refugees in Moldova through coordination with civil society, local municipalities, and donors, the consortium ensured that only the highest priority aid was delivered to support health systems, which remain under significant strain.

With supply chain management and logistics at its heart, the program brought life-saving medical supplies, hygiene items, and durable medical equipment to Ukrainians trapped in the conflict and refugees seeking safety in Moldova and Romania. In all, the consortium moved 514,907 lbs. of aid to over 70 local medical facilities and organizations, which directly helped hundreds of thousands of people.

The collaboration with Tzu Chi proved so successful and valuable to the NGO community that an additional four nonprofit organizations were brought into the consortium and benefited from this collaboration. The Airlink team and our NGO partner network remain grateful to Tzu Chi for their vision for helping fund its launch and flexibility in expanding the project as it operated. Airlink's nonprofit partners saved more than $774,000 in transportation costs due to the project.

TOP: Ukrainian Refugee Relief in Poznań, Poland, 2023

In January, the Tzu Chi Poznań team cooperated with Poznań Red Cross to distribute supplies such as sleeping bags and food to Ukrainian families who arrived in Poland after October 2022 and urgently needed help. The Poznań team moved the Jing Si Multi-Grain Biscuits to the Red Cross distribution site. Photo: Tzu Chi Foundation

BOTTOM: Ukrainian Refugee Relief in Moldova, 2022

After the outbreak of the Russia-Ukraine war, large numbers of refugees poured in to neighboring Moldova. Tzu Chi was able to provide refugee assistance locally by cooperating with IsraAID. On May 24, a team from Tzu Chi and the United Nations went to the border of Palanca in Moldova to visit cooperating organizations and care for refugees. The photo shows the "Blue Dot", a temporary rest area set up by the United Nations International Children's Fund (UNICEF). Photo: Héctor Muniente

LEFT and RIGHT: Pakistan Flood Relief, 2022

In the flood-of-the-century disaster in Pakistan, Tzu Chi cooperated with Islamic Relief to distribute materials in the disaster area. Food packages, water purifiers, and mosquito nets were distributed in Sindh Province. The staff packed the distributed materials one by one. Photo: Tzu Chi Foundation

2022 Floods in Pakistan:

In 2022, Pakistan experienced the worst flooding in living memory. An estimated one-third of the country was underwater, with more than 33 million people affected. At the time, the UN estimated nearly 1 million homes had been damaged, more than 700,000 livestock were lost, and 2 million acres of crops were destroyed.

In the provinces of Sindh and Balochistan, people were living in roadside spontaneous camps with no appropriate cover. With winter approaching in December, Tzu Chi wanted to send its eco blankets to provide those affected by flood with additional warmth and support through the cold winter months.

With Airlink's assistance in transporting relief goods through its partners Qatar Airways and Skyways, Tzu Chi addressed the urgent needs of the flood-affected people just in time, providing 16,608 blankets to 10,416 families.

In partnership with Tzu Chi, Airlink provided door-to-door support, from picking up relief goods at the point of origin to delivering them to an indicated warehouse at the destination.

Airlink coordinated all the transportation processes, including logistics, shipping, and customs clearance, so the organization could focus on planning the distribution without worrying about transportation. In particular, the affected area was in an area of Pakistan where there are no Tzu Chi branches and volunteers, adding complexity to the aid distribution process, especially in relation to customs clearances. Airlink also provided customs clearance assistance, and Airlink's partner clearing agent in Pakistan helped the cargo to be released smoothly.

Airlink coordinated all the transportation processes, enabling Tzu Chi to direct their energy and time toward identifying and working with local NGOs to plan distribution; these organizations include We Care Foundation, Islamic Relief, Shirkat Gah Women's Resource Centre, Al-Madinah Islamic Research Centre (MIRC), and Camillian Disaster Service International (CADIS) to distribute food and NFI (non-food items) packages to 31,000 families.

Together We Heal:
A Journey of Compassion After Displacement

FR. ARISTELO MIRANDA, MI

Executive Director of CADIS

It is with great honor and humility to share my thoughts on this significant and meaningful event—Tzu Chi Global Refugee Relief Exhibition, a testament to the profound impact of compassion in the face of displacement. As the Director of the Camillian Disaster Service International (CADIS), I extend my heartfelt gratitude for the opportunity to share in the collective narrative of "UPROOTED: Compassion After Displacement." Through this poignant theme, we reflect upon the collaborative journey we have undertaken with the Tzu Chi Foundation, uniting our efforts to sow the seeds of hope and healing for displaced individuals and communities across the globe.

The Camillian Disaster Service International (CADIS), a humanitarian and international development Foundation of the Order of the Ministers of the Infirm (Camillians), has been a not-for-profit organization in Italy since 2016. The Camillian, a Catholic Order, was founded in 1586 in Italy by a converted mercenary, Saint Camillus de Lellis, the patron saint of the sick, nurses, and hospitals. Its main charism is to serve the poor sick, even at the risk of our own lives. The Camillians are engaged in healthcare ministry in 42 countries. The Camillians have

shown their commitment and testimonies of taking care of sick persons. Many of its members also died in taking care of those infected by epidemics and the wounded during wars.

The inaugural collaboration of CADIS and Tzu Chi began in India in 2020 at the height of the COVID-19 pandemic through the Camillian Task Force (CTF) of India, a CADIS member organization. The inaugural project delivered relief (food, non-food and psychosocial assistance) to over 520,000 individuals in 854 villages across the 13 states of India. The seed of collaboration has borne fruits of sensitivity and solidarity to the plight of the Ukrainian refugees. In May 2022, CADIS and Tzu Chi were engaged in a more dynamic and strategic response to the needs of Ukrainian refugees. Today, both Foundations have delivered relief (food, non-food, psychospiritual support) and recovery assistance (job, shelter, healthcare) to over 300,000 Ukrainian refugees up to the present. Our collaboration has been inspired by the shared values of charity, compassion, respect, human dignity, and interfaith, and is engineered by our unique capacities, competence, and conviction.

Moreover, in our increasingly interconnected world, where people from different religious traditions often live side by side, it is crucial to build bridges that will connect our initiatives, efforts, desire for humanity and a fully ecologically resilient community of persons where understanding and respect animate their lives. Both CADIS and Tzu Chi believe in interfaith collaboration. Both acknowledge that despite the differences in our beliefs, rituals, and practices, we share some values and aspirations that serve as a foundation of our collaboration to effect positive social change in the communities affected by disasters. We share in identifying common social, humanitarian and environmental issues that affect local communities, such as poverty, hunger, homelessness, climate change, discrimination, and more. We unite around these shared concerns and bring unique strengths and perspectives to addressing these issues. We learn together through projects about each other's values, ethics, and the principles that motivate our actions. Thus, we are sending a powerful message of unity and compassion to the broader society, emphasizing that people of different faiths can come together for the greater good.

In our world, where the harsh winds of conflict, environmental upheavals, and socio-economic inequalities uproot lives and dreams, the Camillian Disaster Service International and the Tzu Chi Foundation stand as beacons of light. Our shared commitment to alleviating the suffering of displaced individuals embodies the essence of humanity's resilience and compassion. As we explore the captured moments within this visual art exhibition, we are reminded that amidst the chaos of displacement, stories of courage, unity, and transformation emerge. It is a sign of hope, a sign that ultimately gives meaning and purpose to all our efforts to effect change and transformation of this complex world.

The cooperative process between our organizations has been a symphony of shared purpose and unwavering dedication. Our paths converged with a mutual understanding that healing goes beyond physical aid— it necessitates the restoration of dignity, the rekindling of hope, and the reaffirmation of our shared humanity. Together, we have harnessed the power of collaboration, merging our diverse expertise, resources, and experiences to create a tapestry of support that extends across borders. It is through this synergy that we have been able to amplify our impact and reach those who need us most.

The heart of this collaborative process lies in the stories of courage, unity, and transformation that emerge from the lives touched by our efforts. From establishing secure havens for displaced families to offering critical medical care, education, and psychosocial support, our collective achievements transcend numbers. They exemplify the resurgence of hope and the revival of dreams amid the chaos of displacement. It is in the smiles of children rediscovering their laughter and the strength of communities rebuilding their lives that we find our common ground—a ground that is fortified by our shared commitment to empathy, resilience, and unwavering compassion.

As we gaze upon these evocative images, let us also look to the horizon—a horizon that beckons us to envision a future where the seeds of compassion continue to bear fruit. Our journey together does not end here; it extends into the vast expanse of possibilities awaiting us. The Camillian Disaster Service International and the Tzu Chi Foundation share a profound vision: a vision of a world where no one is left adrift in the storm of displacement, where empathy is a universal language, and where the act of extending a helping hand knows no boundaries.

"The Camillian Disaster Service International and the Tzu Chi Foundation share a profound vision: a vision of a world where no one is left adrift in the storm of displacement, where empathy is a universal language, and where the act of extending a helping hand knows no boundaries."

Ukrainian Refugee Relief in Poland, 2022

TOP LEFT: On June 2, Tzu Chi Warsaw team held a cash card and eco-friendly blanket distribution at the Salesian Church to assist Ukrainian refugees. Alexander, wearing a volunteer vest, was moved by the Tzu Chi spirit of great love and brought his child to help distribute blankets. Photo: Jiajia Lü

BOTTOM LEFT: On June 4, the Warsaw team went to the shelter of Camillian Disaster Service International in Womianki to hold a parent-child gratitude event. Ukrainian volunteer Anastasiia Malashenko sang the song "One Family" in Ukrainian while everyone performed the sign language together. Photo: Xiulian Chu

TOP RIGHT: On June 2, Ukrainian volunteer Lubov, who was a kindergarten principal in Ukraine, always has a smile on her face when checking information for her compatriots. She carefully explains to them in detail in hopes that her compatriots will receive assistance soon. Photo: Jiajia Lü

BOTTOM RIGHT: On August 3, Jing Si Multi-Grain Biscuits arrived in Warsaw. Tzu Chi and Ukrainian volunteers went to the large material distribution warehouse of the Camillian Disaster Service International in Ursus, southwest Warsaw, to assist with unloading the truck. Photo: Tzu Chi volunteers in Poland

In this era of interconnectedness, the challenges of displacement resonate far beyond the confines of a single community or nation. With this in mind, our common vision is to foster a network of support that spans cultures, continents, and creeds—a network built upon the principles of solidarity, compassion, and unwavering dedication. Through shared knowledge, joint initiatives, and continuous innovation, we aim to lead the charge in transforming refugee relief work into a global movement that nurtures resilience and restores hope to the uprooted.

These images depict more than isolated narratives; they encapsulate a broader human experience. They remind us that even within the depths of displacement, the capacity for renewal and transformation is boundless. As we stand before these images, we are called to action—to contribute, to collaborate, and to champion the cause of those uprooted by circumstances beyond their control. As you traverse this exhibition, let these images spark the flame of compassion within our hearts. Let them inspire us to become part of a movement that seeks to heal wounds, uplift spirits, and rebuild lives.

The journey of compassion after displacement is one of shared purpose and unwavering dedication. As we explore the captured moments within these frames, let us be reminded that compassion knows no bounds and that our shared humanity is a force more powerful than any displacement. Let us join hands, organizations, and communities as we work toward a world where compassion is the cornerstone of our response to displacement—a world where no one is truly uprooted because we stand together.

Thank you for creating this journey of compassion after displacement. Together, we can pave a path of healing and hope for those who have been uprooted, and together, we can shape a future where every displaced individual finds solace, support, and a new place to call home. CADIS remains committed and resolute to working together to provide effective refugee relief and resilience building. By working together, we can make a real difference in the lives of refugees around the world and help contribute to finding solutions to the ongoing displacement of persons. We are calling everyone to contribute to this complex but noble mission of accompanying the displaced peoples to a place which they can call home. This can include donating to refugee relief organizations, volunteering your time, or raising awareness about the issue of displacement. Together, we can make a difference in the lives of refugees and help them to rebuild their lives.

Let me end my reflection with a famous African proverb: "If you want to go fast, go alone; if you want to go far, go together." Together we can help build and strengthen the resilience of refugees. While relying solely on our own efforts and resources might seem to work better in the short term, it is the community we build with others that will sustain our initiatives and overcome the obstacles encountered. It might be slower, but it's what will get us far in the end. In this way, all displaced people will be able to live in safety with dignity and determination amid darkness.

As the gunfire and shelling escalate, UNICEF Ukraine is making efforts to build the capacities of NGOs and youth organizations across the country to address the mental health impact of the war and promote the psychosocial wellbeing of those who have been affected by the conflict. To date, more than 4,500 children and adolescents have participated in activities in Kharkiv's metro stations. UNICEF and partners plan to engage around 500 volunteers, educators and psychologists to support children, adolescents and their families on the move. Photo: courtesy of UNICEF

Faith, Vow, and Action

Volunteers give selflessly,
constantly caring for all living beings.
With 'faith, vow, and action'— when disasters strike,
they emerge like Bodhisattvas,
wholeheartedly dedicating themselves to relieve suffering.

— Jing Si Aphorism by Master Cheng Yen

TZU CHI

VOLUNTEERS

Dedicated to Refugee Relief, Advancing with Love

Stephen Huang
Executive Director of Global Volunteers of Tzu Chi Foundation

Since I first met Master Cheng Yen in Hualien in April 1989, I was profoundly moved by Master Cheng Yen's wisdom and compassion. After that, I converted to Buddhism and was given the Buddhist name "Si Xian" (思賢). Since then, I have followed Master Cheng Yen wholeheartedly and unreservedly, devoting myself to Tzu Chi, promoting Tzu Chi's Four Missions and Eight Footprints, and serving as Master Cheng Yen's "feet". Wherever there is a need, I will go there without hesitation.

From 1991, since Tzu Chi's first international relief effort to provide aid in flood-affected Bangladesh, till the end of 2023, it has assisted 133 countries and regions around the world. In addition to providing emergency assistance with food, clothing, blankets, grain seeds, and medicine to disaster-stricken countries, Tzu Chi has also provided assistance by building houses, building schools, giving access to water, and providing free clinics. Although each project is different, the concept of "respecting life" remains the same.

International refugee care is an important part of Tzu Chi's practice of international relief. As Master Cheng Yen's disciple, her words, "When others are hurt, I feel their pain. When others suffer, I feel sorrow," strongly resonates with me. For more than 30 years, I have been blessed to have participated in many international relief efforts.

Stephen Huang has experienced over 30 years of service as a Tzu Chi volunteer and disciple of Dharma Master Cheng Yen. Photo: Shuli Lo

Following the emergency relief principles of "direct, focused, respectful, practical, and timely", Tzu Chi incorporates medical care, education, and humanistic love to its mid- and long-term relief plans. This integrated approach aims to transform the lives of disaster survivors and refugees, helping them to become self-reliant and get back on their feet.

Whether facing the relentless cruelty of natural disasters such as the Eastern China floods, devastating typhoons in the Philippines, tsunami in Sri Lanka, and earthquakes in Haiti, Türkiye and Syria; or the humanitarian disasters caused by wars such as the 911 terrorist attacks in the United States and the Russia-Ukraine conflict, in this turbulent world, Tzu Chi volunteers clad in blue and white are never absent. As Tzu Chi enters its 58th year, I would like to take this opportunity to express my gratitude to all the volunteers who have participated in Tzu Chi's international relief work. I am grateful for their selfless dedication, which has inspired compassion within and brought light to those experiencing dark times.

On October 7, 2023, the war between Israel and Hamas resumed. Nothing is more heartbreaking than the tens of thousands of unarmed civilians being affected by war. Spreading love and kindness, and actively building a bridge of love and support across racial and religious barriers, is the philosophy of action that Tzu Chi volunteers around the world have always adhered to, and what the Master tirelessly teaches. Here, I once again call on everyone to use love and kindness to resolve the current crisis. Otherwise, conflicts and disasters will never subside.

Fortunately, outside of troubled times, great love is eternal. Tzu Chi is like a lighthouse, and the Dharma boat carries hopes of goodness and sails to the shore of peace and love.

Photo: Muhammed Hak

Faith and Action
Must Always Align

FAISAL HU (胡光中)

Director of Tzu Chi Türkiye
The first Muslim to become a Tzu Chi Commissioner

"No one in the world wants to become a refugee, but the reality is that many people become refugees under circumstances that are impossible to prepare for. This is the responsibility of all people worldwide: we must pay attention to this problem, and let the world know peace and not war."

Earthquake Relief in Southern Türkiye, 2023

During disaster relief distribution in Hatay Province, Kırıkhan, Tzu Chi volunteers met Mr. Erkan (a disaster survivor, fourth from the left) and his family while surveying in Kırıkhan. After understanding their situation, Tzu Chi immediately assisted them with registration, and the family came to the distribution site to receive material aid cards that day. Erkan's 8-year-old eldest daughter, Belinay (third from the left), upon meeting Tzu Chi Türkiye volunteers Faisal Hu and Nadya Chou, affectionately grabbed Faisal's left hand and kissed it. Photo: Wensen Lin

Faisal Hu:

Faith and Action Must Always Align

Faisal Hu was one of the primary forces behind the founding of the El Menahil International School in Türkiye, which provides much-needed education for Syrian refugee children. Syrians speak Arabic, not Turkish, so even if they could afford to enroll in school, it would be difficult to attend a Turkish school. However, there was the issue of being able to afford school in the first place. Adult refugees have a lot of difficulties gaining employment, often working in low-paying unskilled laborer jobs despite being qualified to do much more. Even more devastatingly, refugee children as young as six years old are often used as laborers in factories, since they can fit into smaller spaces, be paid horrifically low wages, and, since labor laws do not apply to them, they can be very easily mistreated by their superiors.

In a talk given at the Tzu Chi Long Island Branch Office, Faisal brought up an example of a Syrian boy who would work thirteen-hour shifts on a daily basis, wherein he would not be allowed to sit and could only have thirteen minutes of break per day to use the bathroom. This child was about twelve years old at the time and had not been able to attend school for over three years. In those years, his suffering was immense.

Faisal reported multitudes of cases similar to the one above to Master Cheng Yen, the founder of Tzu Chi Foundation. He also impressed upon her the fact that most Syrian refugees were extremely reluctant to go to the police even when faced with violence or mistreatment, because they could very easily get deported. Master Cheng Yen said that left unchecked, these refugees, particularly the children, would grow to hate their oppressors and the world, and might ultimately turn to violence and/or crime in retribution. She insisted that these refugee children must be able to have an education which would grant them not only a chance at a better life, but also a feeling of safety and respect, and Faisal wholeheartedly agreed.

The process of making the El Menahil International School a reality was not without its difficulties. Initially, Tzu Chi made agreements with schools that had classes in the morning but were empty in the afternoons to allow the Syrian children to attend school then. However, due to discrimination against Syrian refugees, parents of the school's Turkish students protested having refugee children using the same classrooms as their children, even if their classes were not held at the same time. They held hands and barricaded the schools against the refugee students. For many Turkish people, the Syrian refugees were a scapegoat for why the economy was not doing well. But in the end, compassion and advocacy for the refugees on Faisal's part won, and El Menahil eventually became a reality.

At El Menahil, the curriculum has math, physics, chemistry, history, Arabic, English, and Turkish. They have physical education classes as well. Currently, they are also in the process of adding Mandarin and religious studies (for example: the Quran, Islamic culture, and its principles) to the curriculum.

Faisal is not alone in his endeavors to help the Syrian refugees in Türkiye. Working right alongside him are a number of Türkiye-based Syrian volunteers, all refugees themselves. These volunteers had various professions in Syria before they sought refuge in Türkiye following the outbreak of the Syrian civil war. Before there were schools for the refugee children, they were performing unskilled labor in textile or shoe-making factories and the like. After the schools were established, they came to be teachers and also became Tzu Chi volunteers to give back to the organization which had given them so much.

Faisal's hope for the future is that one day, perhaps twenty or thirty years from now, the alumni of the El Menahil International School might remember that it was Tzu Chi who gave them hope for a better future by creating schools for them. He said he hoped that the compassion and respect given to the students would someday be paid forward by them. But there are plenty of signs that he doesn't have to wait decades to see the fruits of his labor. Just one example is that in the years following the school's establishment, the students and teachers have raised millions of Taiwan dollars for various other Tzu Chi disaster relief missions.

El Menahil International School Construction Survey, 2023

After a meeting with architects, Tzu Chi's construction team went to the new site of El Menahil International School to conduct a site survey. Photo: Jinghui Yang

Fundraising campaign in El Menahil International School in Sultangazi, Istanbul, 2016

Upon learning of the devastation that Typhoon Nepartak brought to Taitung, Taiwan and the frequent natural disasters around the world, Tzu Chi volunteers in Türkiye initiated a fundraising campaign at El Menahil International School in July 2016. The students responded enthusiastically, held up fundraising posters and expressed, 'Seeing the disasters you are experiencing, we feel your pain. We empathize and stand with you.' Photo: David Yu

Early on, Faisal actually mistrusted Tzu Chi, thinking that, as a Buddhist-based organization, it must have some underlying motive behind helping people who were not Buddhist. As a devout Muslim, he suspected that conversion to Buddhism was the organization's ultimate goal. But a single conversation with Master Cheng Yen eliminated that doubt. When the Master was young, she was very poor, and she would have to climb up a mountain to gather firewood each day. On her way, she would always pass by a church, and every day, she would bow deeply before it. She was not a Christian by any means, but she was showing her profound respect for people who were and are Christian. She said that when we remove the boundaries of race, nationality, language, skin color, and religion, all that is left is one word: love. Master Cheng Yen asked Faisal if Islam has love, and he responded that of course it did. One of the many names of God in Islam is al-Wadud, which translates to "The Loving One". The Master then asked if God's love knew any boundaries, and he replied that no, it did not.

Master Cheng Yen asked Faisal if Islam has love, and he responded that of course it did. One of the many names of God in Islam is al-Wadud, which translates to "The Loving One". The Master then asked if God's love knew any boundaries, and he replied that no, it did not.

Faisal stated that one of Islam's core tenets is that your faith or belief and your actions must always aligned. If you believe that God's love knows no boundaries and that you are on this Earth to express that love, then you must put it into action. Belief alone is not enough; there must be action. Along a similar line, Tzu Chi's core philosophy is that of putting compassion into action. Compassion is good and noble, but what use is it without action?

When asked what insight he wished to share with you, our readers, Faisal said, "No one in the world wants to become a refugee, but the reality is that many people become refugees under circumstances that are impossible to prepare for. This is the responsibility of all people worldwide: we must pay attention to this problem, and let this world know peace and not war."

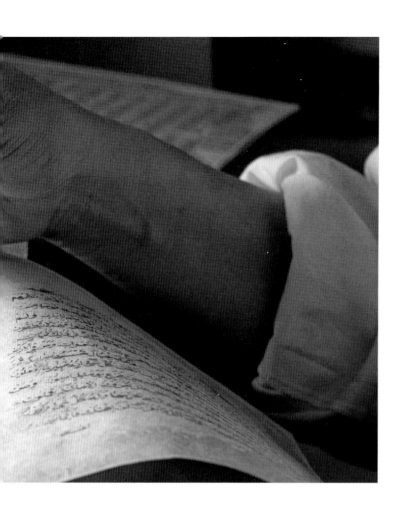

Restoration of a 500-year-old Quran

LEFT: Tzu Chi volunteers in Türkiye, Faisal Hu and Nadya Chou, discovered a 500-year-old hand-copied Quran from an antique books and cultural relics market in Istanbul and presented it to Master Cheng Yen. Due to its old age, the book was filled with dust and mold, and was sent to the National Taiwan Library for restoration. The book restoration team carefully matched tools to adhere the 'classic fixtures' inch by inch, reinforcing and protecting the original pages of the Quran; they also produced a replica while simultaneously repairing the original, binding it by hand with linen thread. Photo: Tzucheng Liu

TOP: The original pages were eroded by insects, soaked in flood water, and the paper crumbled and broken, with each page in tatters. The book restoration experts at the National Taiwan Library carefully searched for similar paper materials, choosing the seven-year-old raw hemp paper for the repairs of the old pages. Photo: Jinghui Yang

Along a similar line, Tzu Chi's core philosophy is that of putting compassion into action. Compassion is good and noble, but what use is it without action?

Protecting Every Flower in the Oasis

Nadya Chou (周如意)

Tzu Chi Volunteer in Türkiye

"On this land,
we stand united with them.
Their sorrow is ours."

Nadya Chou:

Protecting Every Flower in the Oasis

In 1996, Nadya Chou moved to Türkiye with her businessman husband Faisal Hu. Türkiye then became their second home. When Türkiye was struck by a devastating 7.4 magnitude earthquake in 1999, the couple met a Tzu Chi rescue team from Taiwan that had arrived to aid the victims. The universal teachings of love and compassion found in both Buddhism and Islam inspired Chou and Hu to actively participate in the Tzu Chi disaster relief operations. They subsequently emerged as key members of Tzu Chi's volunteer community in Türkiye.

As the Syrian civil war intensified in 2014, a surge of refugees entered Türkiye. Nadya saw Syrian refugee children roaming the streets of Istanbul, begging, scavenging through trash bins for food, or being forced into child labor. During one relief effort, she noticed refugees wanting to trade blankets provided by Tzu Chi for money to cover their children's education. Memories of the tragic aftermath of the earthquake 15 years prior resurfaced, filling Nadya's eyes with tears. Reflecting on the situation, she felt, "On this land, we stand united with them. Their sorrow is ours." Motivated by this, she made a heartfelt commitment to help the begging Syrian children become students equipped with backpacks, ready for school.

The seed of this wish grew in her heart and transformed into strength and action. Together with her husband and David Yu, who is also another Taiwanese volunteer in Türkiye, and other Syrian volunteers, they went from house to house in the evenings, identifying out-of-school refugee children, registering their details, and reporting it back to Tzu Chi in Taiwan. In 2015, with the collective efforts of Tzu Chi and other community contributors, the first refugee school in Türkiye — El Menahil International School — was established. "El Menahil" in Arabic means "oasis in the desert." Starting with support for over 500 refugee children, the school has now grown to accommodate more than 3,000 students. Throughout this journey, Nadya, like a loving mother, has been protecting the blooming smiles of these children in this oasis.

"She binds us together, teaching us the essence of being human. She treats us as her own, just like we are her children. We always eagerly await our meetings with her, counting the minutes, as if writing a book filled with love—documenting all her kindness to us," a poetic letter from a student of El Menahil reveals the sincere heart of this motherly figure towards the refugee children.

Looking at the students studying peacefully in the school, Nadya feels great happiness for them from the depth of her heart. She understands that the path to a peaceful and bright future for these refugee children is long. However, she believes that teaching children about "love" and "kindness" is the beacon that can light any dark path. Today, her compassionate gaze has an added layer of determination.

TOP RIGHT: Earthquake Relief in Southern Türkiye, 2023

From March 5, Tzu Chi distributed aid for four consecutive days in the severely affected area of Nurdagi, a town in Gaziantep Province, benefiting 1,565 households 6,224 people. Nadya Chou, although busy with the emergency relief distribution, still made time to go online and accompany the class of El Menahil International School. A young disaster victim also studies by her side, hoping to own a computer one day. Photo: Mohammed Nimr AlJama

LEFT: Syrian Refugee Home Visit in Sultangazi, Istanbul, 2014

(Second from left) Syrian elder Hussein, Faisal Hu and Nadya Chou visit Syrian refugees who fled to Türkiye due to war to understand the schooling situation of primary and secondary students and assess the distribution of educational grants. A child takes the volunteers back to their home. Photo: David Yu

The following is an interview with Nadya Chou by Tzu Chi Center (TCC), edited and approved by the interviewee before publication:

TCC: You have introduced humanities courses, including ikebana (flower arrangement) and tea ceremonies, especially for students from grades 7 to 12 at El Menahil International School. In a school primarily addressing the survival needs of refugee children, what inspired you to introduce these seemingly "luxurious" and "romantic" courses? And how do students respond to them?

Nadya: I recall the first time I learned ikebana, my teacher created a simple arrangement using just three items and told me, "Ikebana can be expensive, so we grow our own flowers for it." The second time, Tzu Chi volunteer, Sister A-Li, shared her experiences with me. She had little time to teach me, and only emphasized that no matter what we do, the most crucial purpose is to provide "companionship" for the refugees on this difficult life path.

When I returned to Türkiye, following some political changes after the coup, schools sponsored by NGOs could no longer be directly supervised; they were now managed by the government. Our school was no exception, so we couldn't see the students, even though they were our aid recipients. At that time, Tzu Chi had just opened

a free clinic in Türkiye, and the basement of the clinic served as our office and distribution center. That's where I recruited the first batch of students for our humanities classes. We held daily classes for ikebana, tea ceremony, and Mandarin Chinese. Although we had only a few dozen students, they were very sincere. Through these classes, I taught them etiquette, giving them a strong understanding of our humanistic culture. I also taught sign language, storytelling, and accompanied them to the clinic to serve patients. Even if patients didn't understand our sign language, they could feel our sincerity.

Moreover, for our monthly distributions, I'd lead these children to help with me, and over time, they've grown a strong volunteer spirit, arranging shoes, washing dishes, and cleaning. When these students were

transferred to Turkish schools, we had to recruit new students for these humanities courses.

I later started additional classes to continue teaching ikebana and tea ceremony, with teachers from the school also attending. Some children came to class with smiles on their faces, they were polite and kind. They gaze at the beautiful flowers I bring, inhale the fragrance, and break into happy smiles. I play some popular music and traditional zither tunes as background music. Step by step, I teach them how to arrange the flowers. When they see the previously bare vase and sponge turn into a beautiful landscape through clever arrangement, the radiant smile on their faces is quite different from when they first entered. It's a kind of joy that comes from the heart, their faces glowing, experiencing the feeling of 'happiness'.

"Teachers at El Menahil School prioritize character over academic qualifications. We also guide students to prioritize character education over academic performance."

El Menahil International School

Founded by Tzu Chi Foundation in 2015, El Menahil International School serves Syrian families displaced by violence and conflict by providing education and support for children, adults, and their families. Photo: courtesy of Tzu Chi Türkiye

Earthquake Relief in Southern Türkiye, 2023

On February 25, Tzu Chi began the first disaster area distribution at the Taiwan Reyhanli World Citizen Center in Hatay Province, benefiting a total of 352 households and 1,552 people. The children at the Center have a close connection with Nadya Chou. Photo: David Yu

I don't specifically distinguish between refugees and other people. I just feel that if someone is willing to learn, I'll teach them. Even though the cost of flowers in Türkiye is relatively high, I think it's worth it. As for the tea ceremony, even though it's not expensive, it still requires dedication to learn the art. When you see students respectfully serving tea and snacks to us or guests, you can't help but admire what good and courteous children they are. These are the children nurtured by the humanistic culture and spirit of Tzu Chi.

Additionally, Jing Si Aphorisms are a very important part of the curriculum. They learn the teachings of Master Cheng Yen and incorporate these principles into their daily lives.

TCC: El Menahil International School currently has 140 teachers, many of whom are Syrian refugees forced to flee to Türkiye. In my view, this school is not only a home for over 3,000 displaced minors but also provides a stable employment environment for the teachers. Having the same roots and backgrounds, they can deeply empathize with the children's experiences. In the El Menahil 'community', the teachers are also undergoing new life journeys. Could you introduce to the readers how the school cares for and nurtures these Syrian teachers? Could you also share a story or two about some of the teachers?

Nadya: El Menahil School in Sultanghazi has nurtured many Syrian teachers, allowing many Syrian teachers to regain their dignity and continue teaching. For example, we reserved the largest and best classroom to serve as a teachers' lounge. There is a marble balcony outside for teachers to have coffee and enjoy the view because we believe that only teachers who feel loved and have a heart full of love can love children and give them plenty of love.

Teachers like Kinda Aleid and Aboulmalek Wais, after two years of training at Tzu Chi University, passed the Mandarin language exam and received certificates. Whenever Aboulmalek Wais has an opportunity, he uses Mandarin to express his love and gratitude for Tzu Chi. I am also very grateful that he applies what he has learned, transforming knowledge into value. Teachers at El Menahil School prioritize character over academic qualifications. We also require students to prioritize character education over academic performance.

TCC: In a previous interview, you said your dream is for every child to happily carry a school bag to school. I've also seen letters from children to you saying that you treat them like normal kids, as if they were your own. This is the best respect for the children, and it is extraordinary love and wisdom! At the same time, I believe adults and children nourish and learn from each other. Can you share some stories of children that made you proud, touched, or prompted you to reflect and change?

Nadya: Every child has touched me in some way because everyone has a story behind them; it's just a matter of whether the children are willing to talk about these stories. I am delighted to be their Mandarin teacher, teaching them not only the language but also the spirit of Tzu Chi and Chinese culture. In my current Mandarin class, there is a pair of sisters; Ola and Rana Al Katea. They frequently tell me, "Teacher, I love you." Every time I see their smiling faces, I feel very close to them. Another student is Hanan Homada, I assigned her a lengthy Jing Si Aphorism to memorize last year. To my surprise, she mastered it, earning my admiration. So, this year I challenged her with even tougher sentences, and she was willing to take on the challenge and elevate her learning.

There are also students, Rayan Jhpjaiy and Haifa Kahwatie, who work part-time after school to help with their family finances. But when it comes to Mandarin class, they try their best to attend. They work from morning till afternoon then delve into learning Mandarin. One even works after finishing class. Their persistence is heartwarming to see and touches me deeply."

This year, these students all passed the Mandarin proficiency test and received the Mandarin proficiency certificate from the Ministry of Education in Taiwan. This has given us, the teachers and students, great encouragement. They are very diligent; now, in addition to Arabic, Turkish, and English, they also know Mandarin. This has broadened their horizons and made them global citizens.

TCC: Over the years of international disaster relief and refugee assistance, you must have encountered many distressed female refugees. They often face even more severe survival challenges than men and feel more powerless to make choices. How does Tzu Chi encourage and help them? As a senior and beloved female volunteer, do you have any thoughts to share with our readers?

Nadya: Yes, I've heard many stories from female refugees, where blood and tears make up the stories of their lives. For example, there was a pregnant mother, with her congenitally ill son, who fled across the border into Türkiye. She described how she first jumped over the border trench, and after pulling her seven-month-pregnant body up, she then pulled her son out. When they reached Istanbul, they initially had nowhere to stay and later lived with relatives. When she showed me her children, she was so proud. I will never forget her strong eyes and smile!

It's because she safely brought her children here and survived. As a mother, this is immensely admirable and resilient. I am proud of this mother.

I often hug these women, whether during distributions, home visits, or when I see them crying. I know that a warm embrace is worth a thousand words. Tzu Chi Foundation helps eight thousand refugee families in Sultangazi each month, and every family has a woman striving to support it. I often encourage them, saying women can hold up half the sky.

I am grateful to Tzu Chi for giving me the opportunity to help these women and families, including teaching their children Mandarin. My efforts warm their lives, and I also feel fulfilled. There is a Jing Si aphorism, "Helping others is helping oneself." To accompany these Syrian countrymen, I learned about the tea ceremonies and flower arrangement — things I had never learned before. Even if my skills and experience are not one-tenth of true masters, I still feel joyful, doing my best to accompany and comfort them until they find their way to the home in their hearts.

El Menahil International School

El Menahil International School has helped thousands of Syrian refugee children in Türkiye to regain access to education. In the school, we can see the innocent warm smiles and happiness on the faces of the children. Photo: courtesy of Tzu Chi Türkiye

Walking on the Path of *Helping Refugees*

Shu Wei Chen (陳樹微)

Tzu Chi Volunteer in Germany

"War is cruel to the innocent... We are here to help. We hope that these people won't feel hatred, or only know the cruelties of war, but see that there are people who care about them."

Refugee Camp Winter Distribution in Opovo, Serbia, 2023

Tzu Chi volunteers in Europe continue to care for refugees from various countries stranded in Serbia. With temperatures in Serbia hovering around zero degrees Celsius in February, Tzu Chi volunteers visited the refugee camps between February 9 to 11 to distribute winter clothing and donate blankets. Volunteer Shu Wei Chen drapes a blanket over a refugee friend. Photo: Dejan Aksentijevic

Shu Wei Chen:

Walking on the Path of Helping Refugees

Shu Wei Chen, who had been traveling with her German husband, Rudi Willi Pfaff, to Serbia to care for international refugees since 2016, is all too familiar with the brutality of war and the suffering of refugees. "My husband died of cancer, but before he died, he told me in the ICU that he wanted me to continue to do Tzu Chi's work, including his share. Shortly after my husband's passing, the Russia-Ukraine war broke out, and Master Cheng Yen told me to 'pack my bags' and go to Poland." With the rich experience of serving refugees and her late-husband's blessing, this recently widowed 64-year-old housewife, picked up her thoughts and grief and traveled from Germany to Poland.

After nine hours on the road, she became the first Tzu Chi volunteer to enter Poland: "Most of the people who escaped were women with children. Seeing them helped me realize my blessings. My husband had stage 4 cancer, so I was prepared for his passing, but it's not the same for them. With their young children, maybe today, tomorrow, or whenever, they will receive news of their husband's death on the battlefield. Knowing this, I am grateful that I can be with these women. It's really tiring, but I don't think about the difficulties I encounter, I just think about doing as much as I can."

After arriving in Lublin, Shu Wei Chen immediately took the lead. She visited the headquarters of Caritas in Poland every day, taking great pains to introduce Tzu Chi to the public. Initially unfamiliar, they quickly crossed the language and religious barriers to launch large-scale emergency relief, and now Caritas has taken Tzu Chi as its family, and has further promoted mid- and long-term refugee services, focusing on the elderly and disadvantaged families. "We distribute supplies to the elderly three to four times a month, and for those with mobility problems, students and Caritas volunteers deliver the supplies directly to their doorsteps. I'll be going to Lublin again soon. UNHCR has seen the cooperation between Tzu Chi and Caritas, so they hope we can expand our distributions to elderly refugees in the areas around Lublin. We need to accelerate our efforts to train more local students to become our volunteers."

Every trip to Lublin is an expedition. The intensive travels over this period have taken a toll on Shu Wei's back and heels. Nonetheless, she remains committed to aiding the refugees, walking with determination, no matter how slow.

The outbreak of war has been most challenging to the elderly, facing language barriers and health problems. It was much easier to see doctors back in Ukraine, they could just call and book an appointment for the next day. But here, it can take up to six months to a year to get an appointment with a specialist. Additionally, they don't know how to communicate with the medical professionals. On top of this, they can't work, don't have enough strength, and employers won't hire them. Transportation is also a problem, as they can't even read the bus stop signs. It's a foregone conclusion that they'll have to stay in Poland for a long time, but with everything so unfamiliar and so much to learn, and with family scattered elsewhere, these elders no longer dared to take a single step out of the doors of their host families.

Long-term fear, anxiety, and loneliness have led refugee elders into increasing despair. At the end of September 2022, Polish volunteer Hanna proposed to set up the "Dumpling Club", inviting the elderly to come to Tzu Chi's office to make Ukrainian dumplings (varenyky)

on Fridays. This club has since become one of Tzu Chi's mid- and long-term companion programs for Ukrainian refugees. Because of the care and companionship of Shu Wei and others, these dumplings with the taste of their hometowns have gradually brought them out of their despair, adding radiant smiles to everyone's face.

The formation of the Dumpling Club has given these seniors the courage and confidence to reach out to others. 80% of the dumplings are sold for charity, and the Polish Union in the office buys them and puts them on their website. The dumplings are filled with cabbage and flavored with fried cheese, fried onions, mushrooms, or mashed potatoes. There is also fruit sauce flavors, with sour cherries as a specialty! Polish people have never eaten sour cherry dumplings, and they are very impressed, so they always come to buy some. The money from the fundraisers is divided among these elderly. Although it's not much, using their own skills to earn money gives them a sense of fulfillment.

The remaining 20% of the dumplings are donated to Tzu Chi's long-term care recipients, refugees who are unable to work for various reasons, and who are so financially challenged that they cannot afford the luxury of a bag of homemade dumplings. Every time we deliver dumplings to these families, we take pictures and show them to the club members so they may relish the experience as well. The seniors were happy to know that their presence is important and that they can bring some joy to others.

On February 8, 2023, Shu Wei, along with Tzu Chi volunteers from the UK, Italy, and Ukrainian volunteer Sergei from Poland, arrived in the capital of Serbia, Belgrade. Together with twelve local volunteers, they went to five refugee camps to deliver blankets and winter clothes. This will enable the refugees to survive the cold winter and welcome the arrival of spring.

Ukrainian Refugee Relief in Lublin, Poland, 2022

LEFT: To care for people fleeing Ukraine due to the Russia-Ukraine war, Tzu Chi continues to provide humanitarian assistance and care activities in Poland. Tzu Chi, Caritas Internationalis, and Tzu Chi's Ukrainian cash-for-relief volunteers closely cooperate in Lublin to hold dozens of distributions, allowing love to cross religion, language, and race while pooling strength together. Photo: Tzu Chi Foundation

RIGHT: In cooperation with Caritas Internationalis, Tzu Chi carries out the mid-term program, 'Aid for Ukrainian Elders' in Lublin, providing daily living supplies to Ukrainian elders who find it difficult to make a living in Poland. International exchange student volunteers come to the Lublin Provincial Cultural Center to pack and distribute supplies. Photo: Shu Wei Chen

Dumpling Club for the Elderly

In Warsaw, Poland, large sour cherries with sugar are cooking on the stove, ready to be simmered into a beautiful burgundy jam. The sunlight streaming through the window perfectly captures the puffs of flour in the air, turning them into beams of golden sand. Amidst the laughter of the crowd, the air carries a blend of tartness, sweetness, and warmth.

A dozen Ukrainian refugees, their wrinkled hands deftly dividing the fermented dough into small balls, then rolling them into thin round skins, waiting for the cherry sauce to cool down, while sharing their family's varenyky recipe, which has been passed down from generation to generation. When these seniors come here, they become like kindergarteners, competing to see whose dumplings are the best. They fill the thin skins with fillings and thoughts of home and shape them into chubby round or moon-shaped dumplings, arranging them neatly and preparing them for cooking. Volunteers understand the unquestionable pride in the words of these elderly, that is the spirit of more than 400 days of displacement, the family time that they once thought would never change.

Ukrainian Elderly Dumpling Event in Warsaw, Poland, 2022

LEFT: Tzu Chi volunteers initiated a charity sale of vegetarian Ukrainian dumplings, inviting Ukrainian elders to come and make the Ukrainian dumplings weekly, encouraging them to come out of the house and socialize. The elders skillfully knead and roll the dough. Photo: Tzu Chi volunteers in Poland

TOP: The 'Dumpling Club' established by Tzu Chi volunteers has become one of the mid-to-long-term care projects for local Ukrainian refugees. All the food at the Dumpling Club is vegetarian, with cabbage dumplings topped with scallion oil sauce and dipped in yogurt—a traditional way of eating. Photo: Tzu Chi volunteers in Poland

Photo: Courtesy of Monica Chang

Committing to Walk the Snowy Path

Monica Chang (張淑兒)

Tzu Chi Volunteer in Poland

"Despite the fatigue, seeing the smiles of Ukrainians when they receive the Tzu Chi blankets turns all the hardship into happiness."

Ukrainian Refugee Relief in Opole, Poland, 2022

Tzu Chi collaborated with an entrepreneur couple and the government in Opole, Poland, to hold cash card distributions at the Opole Stegu Arena between July 26 to 29 to assist the local Ukrainian refugees. Volunteer Monica Chang's eldest daughter, Olivia (first from the left), also served as a young volunteer, handing over Tzu Chi's eco-friendly blankets to the refugees. Photo: Shu Wei Chen

Monica Chang:

Committing to Walk the Snowy Path

After the outbreak of the Russia-Ukraine war in 2022, many Ukrainians fled their homes to escape the conflict. Poland, a neighboring country, began accepting large numbers of Ukrainian refugees. Monica Chang, a Taiwanese who settled in Poznań, Poland, in 2018 with her Polish husband, Lukasz Baranowski, wanted to help when she learned about the many refugees in need in Poland. Initially, she felt that all she could do was make some donations or give away used items. However, after visiting several Ukrainian groups in Poznań, she realized the complexities and the extent of help needed were much greater than imagined.

Upon learning that Tzu Chi had initiated humanitarian aid for Ukrainian refugees, Monica, who had previously worked at Tzu Chi's Da Ai TV station in Taiwan, contacted her former colleagues and began the journey of relief work. Her call connected her with Shu Wei Chen, a volunteer in Germany, and they began working with Tzu Chi headquarters in Taiwan.

Being parents to three young children and having busy careers, Monica and Lukasz had no experience in refugee aid and didn't know where to start. Monica frequently consulted with Shu Wei, gaining insights from her experiences of assisting refugees in other countries. She discovered several challenges that would need to be resolved. For example, since Tzu Chi was not registered in Poland, there would be potential tariffs or extra fees when importing goods, among other issues that non-local NGOs face.

With her background as a journalist, Monica was used to addressing and solving problems. Through discussions with Shu Wei, they devised strategies to overcome the various challenges. Furthermore, since Lublin in eastern Poland is the first stop for Ukrainians entering the country, the Tzu Chi team in Poland decided to form a partnership with the Red Cross, which has the largest warehouse in Poland.

After reaching a consensus on feasible solutions, the team mapped out specific assistance methods:

1. Emergency Relief into Ukraine: They evaluated sending medical and essential supplies to Ukraine through the Red Cross in Lublin to aid the injured and those in need of support.

2. Humanitarian Care for Refugees in Poland: The plan was to distribute supplies to cities in Poland hosting Ukrainian refugees, ensuring they had food, warmth, and emotional support.

> "Whenever there are differences in opinions, we always discuss them together. I tell the Ukrainian volunteers that both Lucasz and I are Tzu Chi volunteers just like them, so there are no differences in our identities. We are all here to help those in need."

Now, the Tzu Chi team in Poland is well-versed in handling contracts, customs, legalities, government coordination, and shipments. "We negotiated with government agencies, discussed contracts and legalities with different partners, assisted with translations, and meticulously went through all contract terms," Monica shared. She added, "Given the six-hour time difference between Poland and Taiwan, I hardly slept during that period!"

This journey exceeded the couple's expectations, but their desire to help drove them forward. In March and April 2022, they visited shelters in Poznań and made local purchases for donations. Starting in May, Tzu Chi began distributing aid in collaboration with the Red Cross in Poznań and also expanded to nearby cities. During this time, shipments of Tzu Chi supplies and cash cards kept arriving and were stored at their home. Lukasz, a tech company executive, was astonished by the trust Tzu Chi Foundation placed in them. He felt the weight of this entrusted responsibility, valuing and guarding this act of love, ensuring every donated dollar went directly to those in need.

In early June, Tzu Chi, Society of Saint Vincent de Paul, and Bydgoszcz city government, collaborated to hold four distributions in Bydgoszcz. The list of beneficiaries came from the city government's social welfare unit. To ensure the identity of the recipients and track the distribution of the cash cards, volunteers also prepared a register in advance. Those eligible to receive aid also needed to present valid identification to complete the process and receive the cash cards.

Before nine in the morning, there was already a long queue outside the church. Some Ukrainian refugees looked disheartened, while others appeared anxious. One distressed elderly person asked the volunteers if he was on the distribution list and mentioned that he was hungry from queuing up too early. Witnessing all this before her, Monica felt deeply for the damage that war had inflicted on civilians.

Sixty-three-year-old Natalia Shelukhina brought her eight-year-old grandson, Vitalii Chernykh, to receive aid. The boy seemed very anxious. "His parents were killed in the conflict. He has a congenital disease, and his mental state has become even more unstable due to the chaos of war," Natalia shared. The boy, unable to control his anxiety, gripped a volunteer's hand very tightly and would scream if his grasp loosened. Monica and the Ukrainian volunteers tried to comfort the boy and his grandmother with fruits and bread. This grandmother, burdened with the pain of losing her daughter and son-in-law, and caring for a grandson who was unwell, faced endless medical and living expenses. Their future in Poland seemed uncertain. Seeing the departing figures of the grandmother and grandson, Monica and the other volunteers could not help but well up in tears. Wanting to help more, she reported their situation to the city government and marked them for long-term care and follow-up.

Ukrainian Refugee Relief in Poznań, Poland, 2022
On June 10, Tzu Chi Poznań team carried out distributions in the annex meeting hall of the Rokietnica District Fire Department. All the Ukrainian families who came were referred by the Red Cross, with family members having physical or mental disabilities. Tzu Chi volunteer Monica Chang (center) interacts with the children on site. Photo: Jingyan Peng

Regarding the Ukrainian volunteers under the cash-for-work program, the Tzu Chi team in Poland treats them with the same trust and respect. Monica stated, "Whenever there are differences in opinions, we always discuss them together. I tell the Ukrainian volunteers that both Lucasz and I are also Tzu Chi volunteers just like them, so there are no differences in our identities. We are all here to help those in need."

During the distribution, many kind-hearted people proactively offered help, providing venues, assisting in transportation of goods, bringing food and snacks, acting as intermediaries for communication, and seeking resources. Monica said, "Throughout the process, we kept meeting wonderful people, so the more we did the more joy it brought us. Everyone is willing to take on a small part to ensure we achieve our goals." Due to distribution relief work, they have now become good friends and dependable partners, and the Ukrainian volunteers also feel more emotionally connected, realizing they are not alone in this foreign land.

Seeing the physical and emotional effects of war, Monica is more than willing to shoulder the responsibilities of Tzu Chi in Poland, so she can bring confidence and courage for these refugees and enable them to continue living.

Ukrainian Refugee Relief in Warsaw, Poland, 2022

Tzu Chi distributed 45,000 cash cards to Ukrainian refugees. At a distribution on May 6, one recipient said, "My husband and I have eight children. When I heard that cash cards would be given to each family member, I cried with joy. With this card, we'll have enough food for our family for half a year or more." Photo: Faisal Hu

Ukrainian Refugee Aid in Szczecin, Poland, 2022

On June 29, Tzu Chi Szczecin team collaborated with the Oktan-Us Foundation to distribute supplies for Ukrainian refugees. The supplies were provided by Tzu Chi, while Oktan-Us Foundation provided the venue. Ukrainian volunteers distributed candy to the Ukrainian children who came to receive the relief supplies. Photo: Suzhen Wang

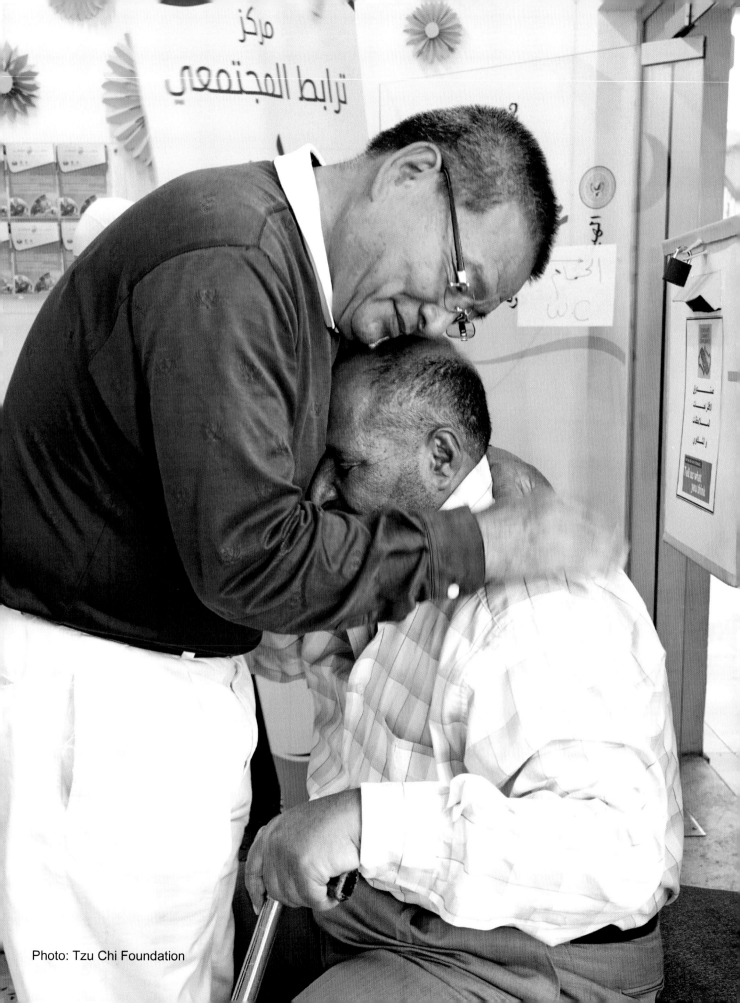

Photo: Tzu Chi Foundation

Giving Endlessly with Love to Drive the Cycle of Goodness

Chiou-hwa Chen (陳秋華)

Tzu Chi Volunteer
Director of Tzu Chi Jordan

Chiou-hwa Chen:

Giving Endlessly with Love to Drive the Cycle of Goodness

We live in a world full of disasters. Since the 20th century, wars have raged in the Middle East. Countries such as Egypt, Syria, and Iraq have continually been engulfed in multiple large-scale wars. Battles between nations have never ceased, leaving countless innocent civilians displaced, desolate, and hungry.

One day at the Ruwaished Refugee Camp on the Jordan-Iraq border, the haunting cries of starving children pierced the air — echoing their terror and extreme hunger. An East Asian man with commanding presence was drawn to these desperate calls. Without hesitation, he rushed towards the wailing cries of despair. Among them, he noticed a severely dehydrated Sudanese child, and without a second thought, he scooped up the child and dashed to a field hospital nearby. Again and again, he tirelessly saved countless children on the cusp of death.

Distribution activities at Za'atari Refugee Camp in Mafraq, Jordan, 2017

LEFT: Tzu Chi volunteers provide care for Syrian refugees who fled to Jordan due to war. They went to the scattered tent areas on the outskirts of the Za'atari Refugee Camp in Mafraq to distribute living supplies to refugee families, as well as to the semi-nomadic Bedouin households of Za'atari. Photo: Xizhang You

RIGHT: The Director of Tzu Chi Jordan, Chiou-hwa Chen, led volunteers in carrying out long-term care for refugees and the Bedouins. Photo: Xizhang You

The Iraq war, which erupted suddenly in 2003 and continued until 2011, brought untold suffering to innocent lives near the Jordan-Iraq border. Among the crowded refugees, people once again saw this East Asian man. He appeared with a rescue team, setting up tents for the refugees living among the ruins. Together with his team, they distributed bread, food, and water to the famished masses. It was clear that this man was no stranger to the plight of refugees. Whether in war-ravaged cities of the Middle East, desolate deserts, or remote mountain villages, wherever there are refugees in need, he is there. Ever-present, ever-smiling humbly, he extends his hand in comfort and blessing. To him, every individual, regardless of their origin or faith, is a life worth cherishing and saving.

People affectionately call this East Asian man "Mr. Chen." He is Chiou-hwa Chen, head of the Tzu Chi Foundation in Jordan.

Chiou-hwa was not always an innate Tzu Chi volunteer with great compassion. Growing up in Miaoli, Taiwan, Chiou-hwa often stood out from the crowd. In 1967, his strict discipline led him to become a taekwondo instructor at a military academy. In 1973, he participated in the inaugural World Taekwondo Championships and was honored as the team captain, later advancing to become a prominent black belt master.

By 1974, he found himself in Jordan, tasked with training the King's guards in taekwondo and fostering the sport's growth in the country. In 1999, following the death of Jordan's King Hussein, Chiou-hwa took on the role of safeguarding Prince Hassan and his family, establishing himself as a trusted advisor and protector. He often jokingly refers to his younger self as "wild and reckless."

Chiou-hwa has always been grateful for his wife's unwavering support of his humanitarian efforts. He remembers being introduced to Tzu Chi in 1997 by her. Knowing that Tzu Chi was primarily comprised of women, he was initially hesitant to join. But his perspective shifted profoundly after meeting Dharma Master Cheng Yen for the first time, leading the once meat-loving and heavy-drinking man to experience a profound transformation.

Chiou-hwa's first contact with Master Cheng

Yen was at a bone marrow donation session as part of the Global Tzu Chi Volunteer Leader's Training organized by Tzu Chi. The challenge of encouraging people to donate bone marrow was like trying to plant willows in a desert. When Master Cheng Yen appeared on stage, he was profoundly moved, as if struck by lightning. This delicate woman had, in 1966, founded a charity and inspired thirty housewives to save 50 NT cents (approx. 1 US cent) a day, collecting it in bamboo banks. Along with five monastic disciples, they sewed an extra pair of baby shoes a day to help the needy. In a materialistic society, she selflessly carved a path of compassion to help those in distress around the world.

As the event neared its conclusion, Master Cheng Yen took to the stage. She spoke about establishing a bone marrow bank, highlighting the immense challenges—not only the need for substantial funding and expert assistance but also the essential need for donors willing to give their bone marrow. From appealing, blood testing, matching, to undergoing bone marrow transplant surgery, there were many uncertainties. If a donor changed their mind at the last moment, all efforts would be wasted.

Chiou-hwa was in shock. It seemed impossible, but Master Cheng Yen's gentle eyes glistened with faith and determination. Despite the challenges, she firmly believed that with the principle of respecting life, compassionate souls would respond.

Master Cheng Yen's words, "respect life," struck him like a hammer, challenging the world that he had always known. Through tearful eyes, he asked himself: "What have I contributed to society in my 47 years of life?" Despite Master Cheng Yen's frail appearance, her aspirations were vast. What was the purpose of his own life?

From that point on, he abstained from meat and alcohol to carry forward Tzu Chi's missions in the Middle East. He had found spiritual refuge in faith, realizing a grand vision of compassion.

Following the US-Iraq war in 2003, Chiou-hwa went to the border between Jordan and Iraq to set up tents for refugees, distribute food, and care for innocent civilians injured by the war. Post-war, many refugees in the Middle East suffered from rare diseases. With profound humanitarian care, Chiou-hwa found ways to provide them with medical assistance, including surgeries. To support the patients' recovery, he not only solicited donations but also covered much of the cost himself. From March 2016 to August 2019, he aided over 1,300 patients, 97% of whom were Syrian refugee children.

To this day, as missiles and gunfire continue to ravage the Middle East, harming countless innocent lives, Chiou-hwa and his volunteer team are once again on the move. Setting up tents for refugees, donating and collecting essential goods, providing emergency food supplies, offering medical assistance, and helping children deprived of education to resume their studies have all become integral parts of his life. For Chiou-hwa, who has spent years shuttling through refugee camps in the Middle East as a leading figure in Tzu Chi, love and compassion are not defined by blood relations. Even the simplest acts of kindness embody an indomitable will, a heroic dream of benefiting the world. He firmly believes, "Giving endlessly with love will undoubtedly set off a cycle of goodness."

Syrian Refugee Relief in Amman, Jordan, 2019
During the Islamic fasting month of Ramadan, volunteers visited the Oula Primary and Secondary School to care for the Syrian refugee (and assisted) students. Teachers and volunteers led the children in dance as everyone brimmed with joyful smiles. Photo: Jin Wang

Master Cheng Yen's words, "respect life," struck him like a hammer, challenging the world that he had always known. Through tearful eyes, he asked himself: "What have I contributed to society in my 47 years of life?" Despite Master Cheng Yen's frail appearance, her aspirations were vast. What was the purpose of his own life?

Becoming Sunshine

Giving Warmth to the Outlanders

Lamiya Lin (林綠卿)

Tzu Chi Volunteer in Jordan

Lamiya Lin:

Becoming Sunshine, Giving Warmth to the Outlanders

"When distributing, please make sure you bow humbly and hand over the supplies with both hands. Make eye contact with them and give them the warmest smile and respect."

Distribution Activity in Mafraq, Jordan, 2023

Tzu Chi Jordan volunteers visit two areas in Mafraq every other month for distribution. In Huweyja village, they distribute food packages to Syrian refugees. Tzu Chi volunteer Lamiya Lin multitasks with recording, photography, and writing to capture the precious moments of volunteers giving bread to children. Photo: Chiou-hwa Chen

An early immigrant to Jordan, Lamiya Lin joined the Tzu Chi Jordan branch in September 2020 and began to fully engage in the aid and care of Syrian refugees. Over the years, Lamiya has been accompanying refugee cases for a long time, helping Syrian single mothers to become self-reliant. As a mother of two, she pays more attention to the medical care and education of refugee children.

Lamiya always faces everyone with a smile. Her warmth, sincerity, and strong empathy shine like a ray of sunshine, bringing more warmth and hope to the lives of refugees who have been uprooted in a foreign land.

The following is an interview with Lamiya Lin by Tzu Chi Center (TCC), edited and approved by the interviewee before publication:

TCC: What were your feelings the first time you encountered refugees?

Lamiya: The first time I went to Huweyia village in Mafraq province to distribute pandemic supplies, I was shocked to see that the refugee children were not wearing shoes. Yet the children had genuine smiles on their faces, as if the lack of materials had no impact on them. However, the adults were different; their faces and hands were weathered, looking exhausted and worn out. After receiving the supplies, there was gratitude and kindness in their eyes towards the Tzu Chi volunteers.

When our eyes met, I could feel the hardships they had experienced over the years, the helplessness of fleeing their homeland, and the humiliations of living at the mercy of others. I said to the young volunteers: "When distributing, please make sure you bow humbly and hand over the supplies with both hands. Make eye contact with them and give them the warmest smile and respect." Many people see refugees as a burden. These people have suffered for a long time and have been treated as inferiors. The psychological torment and loneliness of being a stranger in a strange land, along with the hurt of being

looked down upon, is something that those of us living in comfort cannot imagine. Although they don't express their insecurity, it pierced my heart.

TCC: Over these many years of caring for and aiding refugees, what are the most memorable moments and the toughest times in your memory?

Lamiya: This year, we packed school supplies with the children from "Tzu Xin House", an apartment block of Syrian refugee single mothers and children that Tzu Chi has been supporting since 2013). Even though they are only about 10 to 12 years in age, they know to be grateful to Tzu

Chi and Master Cheng Yen and appreciate the opportunity to do good. As one of the long-term accompanying Tzu Chi volunteers, I feel reassured that the seeds of kindness are being planted in the children's hearts and beginning to sprout. Furthermore, when the mothers from "Tzu Xin House" join us in delivering aid and care to remote areas, they comfort the local impoverished children with a mother's heart. Their benevolent presence is deeply touching.

The hardest yet most enlightening moments are accompanying medical cases, witnessing life and death, and seeing the impermanence of life. Watching a 14-year-old refugee child suffering from osteosarcoma (a type of bone cancer) pass away, hearing the cries of his mother mixed with the cold desert wind, was heart-wrenching. This made me realize how our lives hang by a thread, and arguments about right or wrong are inconsequential compared to the frailty of life.

I have also witnessed loving couples who couldn't grow old together, but they were happy because they deeply loved each other until death separated them. These people serve to teach us important lessons. In the last moments of their lives, they connected with me, entered my life and made me deeply grateful for them.

TCC: Among the Syrian refugees in Jordan, there are many women and children. As a woman yourself, what are your thoughts on their current situation?

Lamiya: Single Syrian mothers, in the absence of their husbands, must also take on the role of the father, providing for the family while educating their children. Beyond worrying about their livelihood and the education of their children, they can be said to have sacrificed their lifetime of happiness to protect and accompany their children as they grow. The carefree life they once had as simple housewives will never return. As refugees in a foreign land, all they can rely on are their own hands.

Starting in May 2022, Tzu Chi Jordan began offering four different vocational training courses for the mothers at "Tzu Xin House". The aim is to enhance their employability so they can work and support their families. At the same time, they can also serve as good role models for their children, teaching them the importance of self-reliance.

TCC: In recent times, what new developments have occurred in Tzu Chi Jordan's efforts to aid and care for Syrian refugees?

Lamiya: In the regions of South Za'atari and Amman, we've been providing care for underprivileged families, some for as long as eleven years. Their children have adapted to the Jordanian environment, with many having completed university education and started working. Thus, starting in May 2023, our volunteer team began conducting home visits to get an in-depth understanding of each family's current conditions. If a family already has the capability to be self-reliant, we will end our monthly support for them and redirect the aid to other families in urgent need. For families without any income, such as the elderly, disabled, or otherwise, Tzu Chi will continue its care and support. With many international organizations shifting their focus elsewhere and the situation for the refugees still just as challenging, this becomes especially brutal for families with no means of livelihood.

TCC: What are your expectations for future refugee care and aid?

Lamiya: Medical care and education will be the continuing focal points. Only through education can the next generation turn their lives around. Living in poverty and illness is genuine suffering, so our free medical outreach program won't be interrupted, with the primary focus being on children under 18.

Children are the hope of the future. It's important to educate them, cultivate compassion, teach gratitude, and guide them to embrace different cultures with an open mind and empathy, as well as with the right faith and mindfulness. Simultaneously, we hope that the Syrian children growing up in Jordan can better integrate into the Jordanian society and pay it forward to help others in the future.

TOP: New Classroom for in Huweyja Village in Mafraq, Jordan, 2021

The tent area in Huweyja village in Mafraq, managed by Teacher Khadija, saw an increase to 43 Syrian refugee families along with an increase in the number of children, making the original teaching space insufficient. Tzu Chi Jordan decided to donate a prefabricated classroom and two toilets to provide the children with a safe learning environment. After two months of preparation and nearly a month of preliminary work, on August 12, the opening ceremony for the prefabricated classroom in Huweyja was held. The opening ceremony was hosted by Lamiya Lin (first from the right) and Chiou-hwa Chen (second from the right). Photo: Tzu Chi Jordan

BOTTOM: School Supplies Distribution in Jordan Valley, 2023

With school starting soon, on August 8, Tzu Chi Jordan volunteers went to three areas around the Jordan Valley to distribute school supplies and new backpacks to disadvantaged students. Later in Karima village, Tzu Chi volunteers delivered stationery sets and backpacks to the children to encourage them to learn. Photo: Jin-Mei Liu

Photo: Asmaa Akhras

Crossing a Forbidden Road

with Love

Mohammad Khair Roz (محمد خير الرز)

Tzu Chi Volunteer in Jordan
Manager of Tzu Xin House

"Since the war, all Syrians have realized how precious it is to feel safe. When we feel confident that we can go back to our homeland and live in safety, we will go back, even if it means living in a tent. We want the war to stop and peace to return."

The vast green land out there, outside of the car window, is Syria. Photo: Mohammad Fayoume

Mohammad Khair Roz:

Crossing a Forbidden Road with Love

"Look! That's Syria!" Mohammad Khair Roz, a Syrian volunteer, pointed to the land on the other side of the border post in Jabir, Jordan, and excitedly said to Tzu Chi Jordan volunteers Lamiya Lin and Khader Khalifeh, who were traveling with him. "Quick! Take my picture!" Tears welled up in his eyes as he spoke, pointing his finger in the direction of his home and country, which he longs for but cannot return to.

February 28, 2023 was an unforgettable day for Mohammad and a major milestone for Tzu Chi. Three weeks after the Türkiye-Syria earthquakes, with the help of the Jordanian military, Tzu Chi was able to successfully coordinate the delivery of two truckloads of the clothing and blankets to Syria. These items were donated by Camel Textile of Taiwan's Kuo Hua Textile's Jordan branch to Tzu Chi. This is the first time that Tzu Chi's supplies have successfully entered Syria. Although it was only a 10-minute drive between the border and the warehouse, it was a breakthrough in the history of Tzu Chi's disaster relief efforts.

Mohammad's father was born in the slums of Damascus, Syria, and made his living as a shoe repairman, but he studied hard and eventually earned three bachelor's degrees in Arabic literature, Islamic law, and law. His father later became a famous scholar at the University of Damascus. When he died, half the population of Damascus took to the streets to attend his funeral. "My father's story encourages me to study and work hard," Mohammad says.

After the Hama political crisis broke out in Syria in 1982, Mohammad left his hometown for Dubai in 1990, where he worked as an Arabic teacher for 17 years. In 2007, he returned to Syria to open a publishing house. Then, four years later, in 2011, the Syrian war broke out. After trying unsuccessfully to find a job in Dubai, Mohammad brought his family to Jordan. The family initially lived together in the Za'atari refugee camp before moving to Jordan's capital, Amman.

It's been 12 years since Mohammad set foot in his homeland. To him, the once beautiful and rich country, one of the oldest cradles of human civilization in the world, has been destroyed and lost all its resources after 12 years of civil war. And now the tables have turned, and Syria now relies on others for food and clothing.

In 2012, four wealthy Syrian businessmen rented 22 apartments on the outskirts of Amman to house widows and their children who had lost their husbands in the civil war. They named the building Beit Safout (Home in Safout). Everyone thought the war would end soon, but in 2016, there was no sign of it stopping. The businessmen had become refugees, and it was getting harder and harder for them to survive, so they looked for ways to get help. Through Tzu Chi

Periodic Relief Distribution of Supplies in Mafraq, Jordan, 2022

Tzu Chi volunteers arrived at the tent area in Huweyja village, Mafraq, to distribute supplies to the Syrian refugees. Volunteers delivered goods such as eggs to the refugees, and Tzu Chi volunteer Mohammad Khair Roz gave toys to the children. Photo: Asmaa Akhras

volunteer Lattefa Lai's introduction, in December 2016, Tzu Chi Jordan's volunteers brought food supplies there for the first time. At the time, Mohammad oversaw the building.

"The first time I came in contact with Tzu Chi, I felt that this charity organization was very different. You can feel that they really care about you and treat other people's children as their own." After the first meeting, Mohammad asked if Tzu Chi could come back next month. Life at Beit Safout gradually stabilized after Tzu Chi began subsidizing the rent as well as providing free medical consultations, food supplies, and sponsorship of tuition fees, etc. In 2017, the building was renamed as "Tzu Xin House" (Home of Compassion). Under the guidance of volunteer Chiou-hwa Chen (Director of Tzu Chi Jordan), Mohammad also became a Tzu Chi volunteer.

With the help of Tzu Chi volunteers living in Jordan, 33 families have moved into Tzu Xin House. In addition to providing them with educational and medical assistance, Tzu Chi has also organized four vocational training classes for single mothers: tailoring, hairdressing, home care, and cooking. As the saying goes, teaching a man to fish is better than giving him the fish, and these skills will enable them to lead a self-sufficient life in Jordan.

"In the past, I had been in contact with other charitable organizations, but I always felt that there was something missing. It was not until I took part in a distribution organized by Tzu Chi that I discovered the difference. The volunteers kept thanking the recipients for accepting our supplies, and that is what giving should be like. I learned the true spirit of charity and how to make genuine connections with people."

On February 6, 2023, a major earthquake

devastated southeast Türkiye and northwest Syria. Tens of thousands of people lost their lives. The powerful quake destroyed thousands of buildings, and those lucky enough to escape were left exposed to the cold, harsh winter weather. With no water, electricity, sufficient warm clothing, and food, life became exceptionally difficult.

After more than a decade of armed conflict between the Syrian government and the opposition, 4.1 million people in Northwest Syria were already dependent on humanitarian aid. In the aftermath of the earthquake, the central government of Syria demanded that all relief operations and supplies be left to their discretion; the complex political environment caused the humanitarian crisis in the Northwest to reach its highest level with the Syrian people becoming innocent victims of the political tug-of-war.

"The day after the earthquake, when I came to the office, I was surprised to find that Mr. Chen had already begun planning to find supplies to send to Syria. When he said that we could start packing the supplies purchased by Tzu Chi, not only was I excited, but the mothers and children of Tzu Xin House were also very excited. We can finally do something for our compatriots in Syria," Mohammad recalled. As he recalled the scene, he couldn't stop the joy from lighting up his face. From February 19, a total of 18 mothers and children from Tzu Xin House spent five hours a day packing supplies for Syrian survivors in the quake-stricken region. When volunteers asked the children if they were tired, they said, "We are willing to work hard for the survivors because we are one family. Although Syria is only a vague homeland for many of the young children, under the nurturing care of Tzu Chi, the seeds of selflessness and love are planted in their young hearts.

On February 28, four military trucks with Tzu Chi's logo on them carried the first batch of supplies to the Jabir Border Crossing, 15 kilometers away. Tzu Chi volunteers Lamiya Lin, Khader Khalifeh and Mohammad Roz stood at the border post and watched as the trucks slowly entered Syria. Although the Tzu Chi banner had to be taken down before entering Syria, and due to policy constraints and security concerns, Tzu Chi volunteers were unable to distribute the goods in person, it still could not dampen the excitement in their hearts—Tzu Chi had finally entered Syria!

As Mohammad watched the truck enter the border and slowly drive deeper into Syria, he had mixed feelings: "My three sisters are still in Syria, and we haven't seen each other for 12 years. Everything I had in Syria is gone. There is no reason to go back, and if I do, I won't be able to come back." Mohammad voiced the sentiments of millions of Syrians who have fled the country, and every word was heavy. Stranded in another country, Mohammad has settled his heart in the present, for there is more to do here.

While there are borders, love knows no boundaries. In the future, may Tzu Chi be able to walk the forbidden road past the Jabir Border Crossing with love and care.

Tzu Chi Jordan 'Türkiye-Syria Earthquake Relief,' 2023

A magnitude 7.8 earthquake struck Türkiye and Syria on February 6 causing great devastation. The Jordanian Taiwanese Camel Textile donated clothing and blankets to Tzu Chi Jordan, which collaborated with the Jordan Hashemite Charity Organization (JHCO) for the Jordanian military to transport the supplies to the Syrian border. The supplies were then picked up by UN vehicles and taken into Syria to reach survivors in the quake-stricken areas. At noon on February 26, supplies arrived at the JHCO warehouse in Mafraq. Photo: Tzu Chi Jordan

"In the past, I had been in contact with other charitable organizations, but I always felt that there was something missing. It was not until I took part in a distribution organized by Tzu Chi that I discovered the difference. The volunteers kept thanking the recipients for accepting our supplies, and that is what giving should be like. I learned the true spirit of charity and how to make genuine connections with people."

Periodic Relief and Distribution of Supplies in Mafraq, Jordan, 2022

Tzu Chi Jordan volunteers distributed food supplies to 28 Bedouin families in the tent area of Za'atari and to 43 Syrian refugee families in Huweyja village. Volunteer Mohammad Khair Roz interacted with the children of these families. Photo: Lamiya Lin

TOP: Free Clinics and Distributions in Jordan, 2016

Tzu Chi volunteers provide care for Syrian refugees who fled to Jordan due to war, with Tzu Chi volunteers from Taiwan and elsewhere joining forces in Jordan to hold free clinics and distributions. Volunteers went to the tent-scattered areas outside the Mafraq Za'atari refugee camp to care for and distribute living supplies to the refugee families. Women holding the distribution vouchers came to receive supplies. Photo: Debby Pan

RIGHT: Medical Mission by Tzu Chi International Medical Association in Jordan, 2018

The Azraq refugee camp in Jordan is located in a desert area and shelters more than forty thousand Syrians surrounded by circles of barbed wire. Photo: Yao Hua Hsiao

Hearts Full of Warmth

Love is life's greatest treasure.
With love in our hearts,
every story encountered will warm the heart.

—Jing Si Aphorism by Master Cheng Yen

U^PROOTED:

The Exhibition

A young refugee woman with her baby in her arms is walking barefoot through the tents in the camp where she lives. Torbalı district of İzmir, Türkiye, where refugees working as seasonal agricultural workers mostly live in unofficial tent camps in rural areas. In Torbalı, there are at least 26 unofficial tent areas where approximately 20,000 refugees work as seasonal agricultural workers, including 6,000 who have been recently internally displaced due to the destructive earthquakes on February 6, 2023. There are at least 75 children in each camp, deprived of their rights to education, health, sanitation, and other basic human rights. Photo: courtesy of Doctors of the World Türkiye

Walking in the Footsteps of Compassion
— Tzu Chi Global Refugee Relief Exhibition

DEBRA BOUDREAUX

CEO of Buddhist Tzu Chi Foundation, USA

Tzu Chi, guided by Master Cheng Yen's teachings of "unconditional loving-kindness, and universal compassion," has taken initiatives to align with the core principles of the "Global Compact on Refugees" ahead of the 2023 Global Refugee Forum. This underscores our belief that compassion knows no borders, and we are dedicated to alleviating the suffering of those in need. Master Cheng Yen's deep concern for the world motivates us, even though we acknowledge that our contributions may seem small in the grand scheme of things.

The purpose of Buddhism in the world is to follow the Bodhisattva path, and Tzu Chi strives to extend its compassion to all corners of the world.

The Global Refugee Forum, held every four years, is a platform that brings together various stakeholders, from countries and refugee communities to multiple organizations and experts, all with the common goal of supporting refugees. At the 2019 forum, over 3,000 participants made more than 1,400 commitments to provide support in various forms.

In preparation for the 2023 Global Refugee Forum, Tzu Chi has initiated the "UPROOTED: Compassion After Displacement" exhibition at the Tzu Chi Center. This event aims to draw attention to the long-term and equitable hosting of refugees, advocating for shared responsibility and future planning. It is a collaborative effort that requires the involvement of all stakeholders. We emphasize the importance of being prepared, empathetic, and working together to face challenges and find solutions.

Tzu Chi Global Refugee Relief Exhibition, 2023

On June 13, Tzu Chi USA unveiled its global refugee relief exhibition at the Tzu Chi Center for Compassionate Relief in New York City. Tzu Chi USA's Chief Executive Officer Debra Boudreaux warmly welcomed the audience in the opening ceremony. Photo: Enpu Kuo

The exhibition presents the work that Tzu Chi is carrying out in Poland for Ukrainian refugees, the assistance given to Syrians in Serbia, Jordan, and Türkiye, the medical care to refugees in Thailand as well as the physical and emotional support for refugees in Malaysia. A special display of 73 paintings from the children of El Menahil International School in Türkiye reflects their internal transformations from despair to hope. On the third floor, is the story of the Buddha as well as the origins of Tzu Chi and its four decades of humanitarian aid for refugees worldwide.

In the opening ceremony, Darla Silva, Chief Program Officer at UNICEF USA, admired the global movement addressing the international refugee humanitarian crisis. Every photograph, artwork, text, and video in the exhibition, along with their underlying stories, is a testament to the power of compassion. We welcome everyone to join us in making a positive impact and leaving their footprints of compassion alongside ours.

Tzu Chi Global Refugee Relief Exhibition engages with community leaders and puts Buddhist Compassion into action, embodying the values of Respect, Gratitude, and Love for all. Our primary focus is to increase awareness and emphasize the crucial principle of "leave no one behind."

Tzu Chi Global Refugee Relief Exhibition, 2023

More than 70 special guests and Tzu Chi volunteers attended the opening ceremony. In attendance were representatives from UNICEF USA, the Parliament of the World's Religions, CAIPA, Inc., New York City Police Department Community Affairs Bureau, NYS Governor's Office, Buddha's Light International Association, Turkish Cultural Center NY, the Baha'i International Community, the Chan Meditation Center, and more. UNICEF USA's Chief Program Officer Darla Silva (BOTTOM RIGHT) made a keynote presentation. Guests took a tour of all three floors of the building, exploring different parts of Tzu Chi's global refugee relief efforts as well as Tzu Chi's own history and philosophy. Photo: (TOP) Enpu Kuo / (BOTTOM LEFT) Hui Liu / (BOTTOM RIGHT) Héctor Muniente

Each blessing added to the wall creates a beautiful image of positive energy and goodwill, reminding us of the goodness within and around us. Let us come together in compassion and connection to create a testament to the transformative potential of supreme and unconditional love symbolized by the blooming lotus on our wall.

Tzu Chi Global Refugee Relief Exhibition, 2023

Visitors wrote their comments about the exhibition and their blessings to the world on the message wall in the gallery on the second floor, each note representing a petal on a lotus flower. Photo: (TOP) Hui Liu / (LEFT) Hui Liu / (BOTTOM RIGHT) Enpu Kuo

Stability Amidst Uncertainty and Confusion

— Tzu Chi's "UPROOTED: Compassion After Displacement" Exhibition

TING FAN

Director of Culture and Communications Department of Buddhist Tzu Chi Foundation, USA

In February 2019, encouraged by Master Cheng Yen, Tzu Chi USA launched a fundraising campaign for the El Menahil International School in Istanbul, Türkiye. The Tzu Chi USA video production team and I then traveled to Istanbul. Interacting with Syrian refugee students and their teachers at the school left an impression. When the Tzu Chi Center for Compassionate Relief opened in Manhattan in October 2019, I contemplated how wonderful it would be to exhibit the story of El Menahil International School there.

In February 2022, the Russia-Ukraine war erupted, and by April, we journeyed to Poland as Tzu Chi commenced aid efforts for Ukrainian refugees. This endearing group of people had to leave their homes, torn from their roots, while their hearts remained tied to their homeland. Witnessing their struggles and helplessness was heart-wrenching. During our stay in Poland, where Tzu Chi was offering immediate economic and emotional support, I thought, "Could we display Tzu Chi's support

for Ukrainian refugees at the Tzu Chi Center?"

Therefore, when the Tzu Chi Center decided to organize a special exhibition focusing on Tzu Chi's aid for global refugees, my team and I enthusiastically provided our documentaries, photographs, and text, recounting the whole story. I thought, "Finally, in New York, a window to the world, Tzu Chi's relief efforts for international refugees would be seen."

We named the exhibition "UPROOTED: Compassion After Displacement" to portray a positive and hopeful energy. "Uprooted" signifies the involuntary displacement from one's homeland, filled with helplessness and unease. However, "Compassion After Displacement" emphasizes the humanitarian relief actions undertaken by Tzu Chi worldwide over the past 40 years. These compassionate efforts have enabled displaced individuals to establish new roots and start afresh with Tzu Chi's support.

Designer Ling Soo incorporated "Mirror Vinyl" in different sections of the exhibition space. When people walked by this reflective material, they could see their faces mirrored yet blurred, aptly conveying the refugees' perplexity and uncertainty about what lies ahead. Opting for acrylic sheets that naturally and seamlessly blend into the white walls rather than traditional frames allowed the images to expand. This design choice signified that the refugees' future holds infinite hope, unrestricted by boundaries.

While the overall tone of the exhibition reflects the harsh reality of war, the photographs captured moments revealing warmth, mutual assistance, and the empowerment Tzu Chi aims to offer refugees. Seventy-three student drawings shipped from El Menahil International School in Türkiye were a highlight of the exhibition. Each encapsulates a heartbreaking story, merging war experiences and current worries. Yet, woven into the visual narrative, we could see Tzu Chi's presence, awakening hope. Ultimately, the exhibition, which opened on June 13, 2023, aimed to convey how compassion can dissolve despair after displacement and shine a path to a new life.

Tzu Chi Global Refugee Relief Exhibition, 2023

RIGHT: The wall is filled with drawings from students of El Menhail International School to inspire the viewers with the lively expressions from the children after overcoming hardships. Photo: Ting Fan

BOTTOM LEFT and RIGHT: Mirror Vinyl is incorporated in the designing concept. Photo: Philip Hwang

When people walked by this reflective material, they could see their faces mirrored yet blurred, aptly conveying the refugees' perplexity and uncertainty about what lies ahead.

Let Love Flow Endlessly

With hearts filled with compassion,
let endless love transform lives in suffering.

— Jing Si Aphorism by Master Cheng Yen

TZU CHI CENTER

for

Compassionate

Relief

TZU CHI GLOBAL
REFUGEE RELIEF
EXHIBITION

UPROOTED

Compassion
After
Displacement

TZU CHI
TZU CHI CENTER
FOR COMPASSIONATE RELIEF

Photo: Philip Hwang

Home is Where the Heart Rests at Ease

KATE CHAO

Director of Tzu Chi Center

In Manhattan, New York, after turning east from 3rd Avenue onto 60th Street and walking a hundred meters down, you will come across a white five-story building. Compared to the All Saints Episcopal Church on the opposite side of the road and nearby shops, it has no flashy signs nor architectural style. This unassuming structure, known as the Tzu Chi Center for Compassionate Relief, unveils its identity through the Tzu Chi flag gently unfurling in the wind on the third floor. Every time I walk in, Dharma Master Cheng Yen's instructions to me echo in my ears: "This is Tzu Chi's seat next to the United Nations. Take good care of this home."

Manhattan, New York is the global epicenter of politics, economics and culture. Placing a home at this busy intersection carries extraordinary responsibility and significance.

How can Tzu Chi's values be conveyed to society more broadly through this home and connect with people from different backgrounds and religions here in New York and beyond? As a unique global location for Tzu Chi Foundation, Tzu Chi Center was established to achieve the following goals:

1. Serve as Tzu Chi's window to the world, allowing the world to understand and recognize Tzu Chi.

2. Foster partnerships between Tzu Chi and those around the world who share the same philosophy and work together to support humanitarian initiatives.

3. Become a platform for the younger generation of Tzu Chi volunteers to participate in Tzu Chi.

Tzu Chi Center

On June 12, 2023, the "UPROOTED: Compassion After Displacement" exhibition opened at the Tzu Chi Center. On the day of the opening ceremony, Tzu Chi members took a group photo in the courtyard of the Center. Photo: Enpu Kuo

The projects initiated by Tzu Chi all originate from the teachings of the Buddha, aiming to inspire kindness in people, spread the message of love, and sow seeds of compassion and great love. Through this, we strive to build a warm, peaceful, and mutually supportive society. The Center's Chinese name 慈濟大愛人文中心 (Tzu Chi Great Love Humanistic Center) reflects these principles.

People's perception of "Buddhist organizations" often revolves around the idea of personal enlightenment through self-cultivation, with limited consideration of actively integrating individual practice into the ever-changing global community. Since its founding by Dharma Master Cheng Yen, Tzu Chi has been guided by its social mission, transcending religious boundaries, committing to global humanitarian relief, actively participating in issues faced by all humankind, and "putting Buddhism into action." It is precisely for this reason that the Tzu Chi Center for Compassionate Relief in New York symbolizes

Tzu Chi's steadfast strength in society, serving as a place for Tzu Chi's humanistic expression.

On October 13, 2019, Tzu Chi Center officially opened along with the photography exhibition of "Keep Hope Alive: 10 Years of Care in Haiti". Following the COVID-19 pandemic, in September 2022, Tzu Chi Center held a week-long "Holistic Climate Solutions Summit". From June 2023, the exhibition "UPROOTED: Compassion After Displacement" focuses on Tzu Chi's continued international refugee assistance from 1979 to 2023. It conveys Tzu Chi Center's mission to promote the Buddhist philosophy of care and empathy towards people in different circumstances and locations.

The first of the three floors of exhibition content, showcases the plight of Syrian and Ukrainian people displaced by war, the support they have received from Tzu Chi around the world, records of aid given to Serbian refugees, and a timeline of Tzu Chi's international assistance. The second floor displays drawings

Since its founding by Master Cheng Yen, Tzu Chi has been guided by its social mission, transcending religious boundaries, committing to global humanitarian relief, actively participating in issues faced by all mankind, and "putting Buddhism into action."

from Syrian children at El Menahil International School in Türkiye. It reveals their emotional journey from displacement to receiving love and care from Tzu Chi volunteers around the world. The third floor is "Following the Buddha's Direction" and "I Think of My Master", which displays the origins of Tzu Chi and reviews the Buddha's homeland and important milestones in his life.

Beyond the exhibition of pictures and documents of global refugee relief, one touching highlight of the exhibition is the simple yet moving drawings of refugee children from the El Menahil International School in Türkiye, sent from thousands of miles away. These artworks have touched and soothed the hearts of visitors, providing a more intuitive understanding of the mission for the future. I believe these children's drawings contain and convey the desire for a stable home and the expression of beauty and goodness. This is an eternal and universal truth, the root of our souls.

I am grateful for our opportunity to be part of this world of Tzu Chi, to follow Master Cheng Yen and contribute a bit of our effort and care to those in suffering around the world through the sharing of truth, goodness and beauty. "Home is where the heart rests at ease." The world around us is always facing many challenges, just like the constant noise and sirens on the streets of Manhattan. This small white building is filled with the firm belief of Tzu Chi people around the world, allowing the residents of the community to trust it, and allowing Tzu Chi volunteers to feel the warmth and strength of home.

We hope to plant a seed of kindness in all our friends who visit and make Tzu Chi Center a nurturing home for enlightenment. Here, we hope to eliminate the boundaries and barriers between people so that great love can spread far and wide.

Thanks for everyone's support.

Meet and Unite *in* ***Great Love***

Crossing all faiths and boundaries, Tzu Chi volunteers actively mobilize local and international forces, weaving together a more complete and long-lasting network of great love. Whether it is communicating and displaying Tzu Chi's humanistic projects or cultivating new driving forces, Tzu Chi Center has consistently strived to convey Tzu Chi's core philosophy of promoting world progress through love and compassion. This is how the Center has become an indispensable link in this network.

During the "UPROOTED: Compassion After Displacement" exhibition, the Tzu Chi Center organized many activities and received thousands of visits from individuals and groups. United by the shared belief in "Great Love", we meet and are brought together by this spirit as we continue to carry this forward with love and compassion.

Activities at the Tzu Chi Center, New York, 2023

TOP: On the weekend of October 21-22, Tzu Chi Center partnered with Open House New York for the OHNY weekend and offered guided tours, tea meditation and flower arrangement for the public. Photo: Hui Liu

BOTTOM: On September 7, Rey-Sheng Her, Deputy CEO of Tzu Chi Foundation paid a visit to the exhibit and Tzu Chi Center along with local volunteers during his visit to the US. Photo: Yinhsu Liu

Activities at the Tzu Chi Center, New York, 2023

UP: On June 27, students from Tzu Chi University of Science and Technology in Taiwan came for orientation to start their internship. They joined a guided tour of the exhibition given by Tzu Chi volunteers. Photo: Yinhsu Liu

RIGHT: On August 4, children from Brooklyn Tzu Chi Summer Camp visited Tzu Chi Center, and learned how Tzu Chi volunteers practice "Gratitude, Respect and Love" during the relief service through the tour of the exhibition. Director of Tzu Chi Center, Kate Chao, interacted with the students in the tour. Photo: Tzu Chi Center

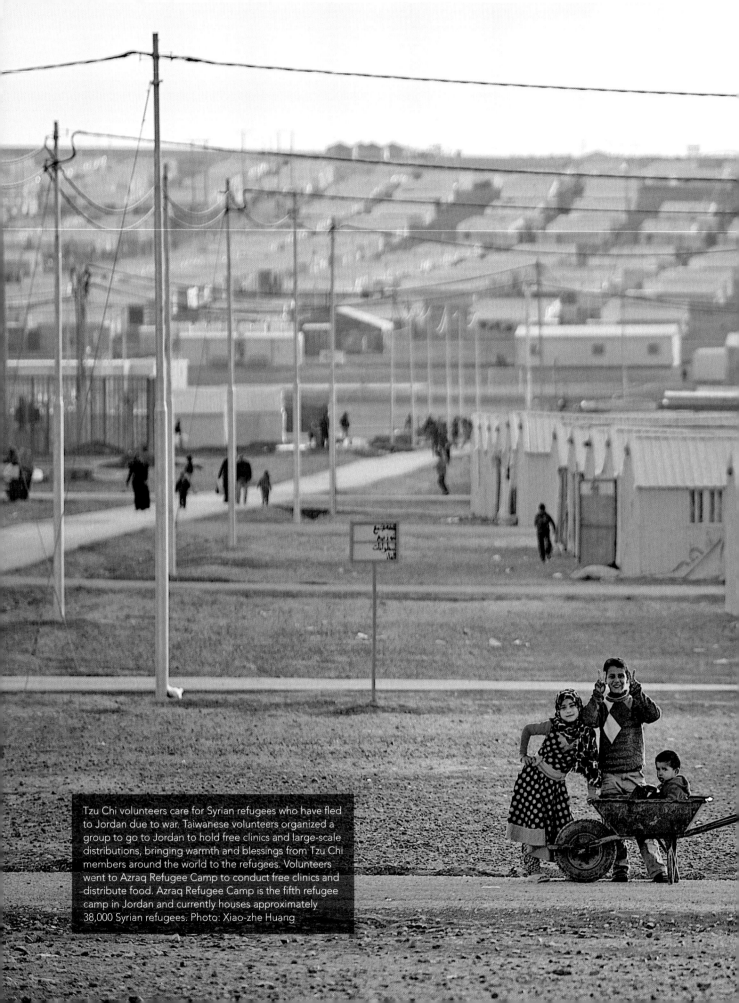

Tzu Chi volunteers care for Syrian refugees who have fled to Jordan due to war. Taiwanese volunteers organized a group to go to Jordan to hold free clinics and large-scale distributions, bringing warmth and blessings from Tzu Chi members around the world to the refugees. Volunteers went to Azraq Refugee Camp to conduct free clinics and distribute food. Azraq Refugee Camp is the fifth refugee camp in Jordan and currently houses approximately 38,000 Syrian refugees. Photo: Xiao-zhe Huang

Only Seeds that are Sown
can Sprout

Teach children to give rise to loving-kindness.
When seeds of goodness are sown,
love will sprout and grow.

—Jing Si Aphorism by Master Cheng Yen

Colors *from*

El Menahil

Drawings by Students
from El Menahil International School, Türkiye

From Desert to Oasis:

A Letter from the Principal of El Menahil

CUMA SERYA

Consultant and Former Principal, El Menahil International School

Indeed, education is what uplifts a generation while ignorance does the opposite. An entire generation of Syrian children in Türkiye is threatened by ignorance and illiteracy.

The sound of that child's crying still echoes in my ears when he was trying to free himself from his mother's grip to go to school along with his older brother, saying, "Why can't I go, too?" His mother's heartbreaking response was, "Next year, you will go to school, and he will go to the workshop, so you can exchange."

Such were the conditions of the Syrians at the beginning of their journey as refugees in Türkiye. Some of the children watched Turkish children on their way to school, while others waited at their doorstep until the school bus left, remembering the days when they used to play and learn in the schoolyards in Syria. Behind them, their mothers hid their tears as they wiped their child's head and said, "You will go to school like them one day, my child."

Indeed, education is what uplifts a generation while ignorance does the opposite. An entire generation of Syrian children in Türkiye is threatened by ignorance and illiteracy.

El Menahil International School

The United Nations International Children's Emergency Fund (UNICEF) donated 6,600 books to El Menahil International School, hoping that the children could enrich their extracurricular knowledge in addition to their standardized studies. Eight years ago, Muhammed Hak roamed the streets until he was found by Tzu Chi volunteers who arranged for him to study at El Menahil. Now, he is preparing for university entrance exams. On July 29, 2022, Muhammed came to the school as a volunteer to read picture books with the children. Photo: Tzu Chi Türkiye

In late 2014, a glimmer of hope emerged during a meeting with Mr. Faisal Hu. After explaining the future risks for the children if they remained out of school, he took the project upon himself and traveled to Taiwan. After lengthy discussions and deliberations, approval was granted for a few students initially. Meetings with the Directorate of National Education in the Sultangazi region took place to discuss the idea of establishing a school for the Syrian students, leading to the establishment of the first branch of El Menahil School in Najib Fadel School.

On the morning of January 23, 2015, we were there early at Najib Fadel School. This date will be long remembered by Syrians. We started with approximately 570 students. What can we imagine about the reactions, emotions, and excitement of the students on that day? Indeed, emotions speak louder than words. Those moments will remain unforgettable forever.

El Menahil is like a cloud of goodness that rained on barren land, creating an oasis of flowers whose fragrance will fill their homeland in the future.

By the second year, we had three schools, with over 2,400 students. With the success achieved, we established seven schools in the third year, with many students, around 3,200 students, and El Menahil later became a model spread across all Turkish provinces.

Amid all these joys, the pains did not end. Many students couldn't attend school as they were supporting their families. It was necessary to find a solution to bring them back to school.

Indeed, we faced a significant problem with these students and their families. How could we bring these students back to school without affecting their family's livelihood? Finally, a monthly salary was allocated for each student who supported their family, with the salary being the same as what they earned from their work.

In 2017, we opened a private, completely free international school where students could acquire knowledge and ethics. This school now hosts around 4,500 students, including the formal education program, weekend courses, and Turkish and English language courses.

If we want to talk about lives that completely changed after they joined El Menahil, look at students like Shaimaa, who lost her father when she was just a baby. After fleeing the war in Syria, she had to work in workshops and give up her dreams. But thanks to the scholarship she received, she is now a student at a top university in Istanbul.

Another example is Fakhri Al-Sheikh Rashid, a student who was out of school for years and worked in factories for a low wage. After joining the school, he received a scholarship and moral support, and he achieved a perfect score in the university entrance exam. He is now a second-year college student.

El Menahil has transformed the lives of an entire generation, transforming them from despair to hope, enabling hundreds of students to enter Türkiye's colleges and universities, learning ethics and science.

Drawings by Students from El Menahil

滿納海學生們的畫

This exhibition showcases 73 drawings from students of El Menahil International School; they are Syrian children who lost their home. In their world, the helplessness they faced, and the imagination of the future are far beyond what was presented in these 73 drawings. Here, we selected a portion to keep in this book. The students are 12 to 17 years old (grade 7 to 12 students). May all the readers truly see, through these colors from El Menahil, the authentic heartfelt expressions deep from the children's hearts.

Drawings by /繪者的名字:

PAGE I: RAYAN ALHAMO
PAGE II: TASNEEM SHARTEH

PAGE III & IV: ROKSANA WOLLOU

نحتاج مساعدة !!

hedige Eburas 81C ♡

PAGE IX: TOP（上）: MARAM BADET

BOTTOM LFET（左下）: MARAM BADET | BOTTOM RIGHT（右下）: WALA ALZIR

PAGE X: NOHA AHMED

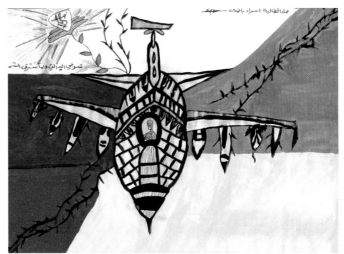

滿納海學生們的畫

Drawings by Students from El Menahil

本次展覽裡共展出了七十三幅學生們的畫作，它們來自滿納海國際學校裡那些失去家園的敘利亞孩子們。而在他們的世界裡，對當下無助感的描繪和對未來想像的圖景要遠比這七十三幅畫裡所呈現的更多。在此，我們精選了一小部分收錄在這本畫冊中，它們由年齡十二歲到十七歲（七年級到十二年級）的學生所繪。願讀者們能夠透過這些來自滿納海的色彩，感受到孩子們最真實的心聲。

From the Hearts of Children

Syrian refugee children attending El Menahil International School – established in 2015 by Tzu Chi in Istanbul, in the Republic of Türkiye – have expressed their stories in these drawings.

Listen to the students share the experiences behind their artwork on our website:

繪者的名字 / Drawings by:

PAGE XI:

1. MUHAMMED SHARTEH
2. MARAM ALZIR
3. MALAK MAAZ
4. ESRAA BAKHET
5. CEDRA SELAMA

1   3

4   2   5

PAGE XII:

6. SIDRA HAJI SALAMEH
7. JESSICA MUSTAFA
8. ROKSANA WOLLOU
9. WEAM ALZIR

6   8

7   9

慈濟國際難民援助特展

根 繫 何 處

——流離失所後的慈悲共渡

二〇二三年六月

編輯：慈濟大愛人文中心
慈濟文史處

BUDDHIST TZU CHI FOUNDATION

書　　　名／根繫何處：流離失所後的慈悲共渡──慈濟國際難民援助特展
出　　　品／沈慈知（慈濟大愛人文中心主任）
策畫指導／蘇煜升（慈濟美國紐約分會執行長）
策　　　畫／葉子
執　　　行／朱苔禎、劉音序
畫冊設計／葉子、李侑蓉、蘇曉玲
封面設計／莫炳燊、蕭明蘭
展覽設計／慈濟美國文史室
責任編輯／葉子、沈昱儀
美術編輯／菩薩蠻數位文創團隊
作者名錄／徐麗梅、唐學慧、蔡苡盈、羅奇華、葉子、王偉齡、林弘展
翻　　　譯／劉音序、蔡苡盈、張裔宗、William James Spencer、葉子
中文審校／江淑怡、楊景欣、周素滿
英文審校／陳尚薇、劉音序、鄭婉琦
資料來源／慈濟數位典藏網、慈濟全球資訊網、慈濟月刊、美國慈濟世界、慈善新聞網
企畫選書人／賈俊國

總 編 輯／賈俊國
副總編輯／蘇士尹
編　　　輯／黃欣
行銷企畫／張莉滎、蕭羽猜、溫于閎

發 行 人／何飛鵬
法律顧問／元禾法律事務所王子文律師
出　　　版／布克文化出版事業部
　　　　　　台北市中山區民生東路二段 141 號 8 樓
　　　　　　電話：(02)2500-7008　傳真：(02)2502-7676
　　　　　　Email：sbooker.service@cite.com.tw
發　　　行／英屬蓋曼群島商家庭傳媒股份有限公司城邦分公司
　　　　　　台北市中山區民生東路二段 141 號 2 樓
　　　　　　書虫客服服務專線：(02)2500-7718；2500-7719
　　　　　　24 小時傳真專線：(02)2500-1990；2500-1991
　　　　　　劃撥帳號：19863813；戶名：書虫股份有限公司
　　　　　　讀者服務信箱：service@readingclub.com.tw
香港發行所／城邦（香港）出版集團有限公司
　　　　　　香港九龍九龍城土瓜灣道 86 號順聯工業大廈 6 樓 A 室
　　　　　　電話：+852-2508-6231　　傳真：+852-2578-9337
　　　　　　Email：hkcite@biznetvigator.com
馬新發行所／城邦（馬新）出版集團 Cité (M) Sdn. Bhd.
　　　　　　41, Jalan Radin Anum, Bandar Baru Sri Petaling,
　　　　　　57000 Kuala Lumpur, Malaysia
　　　　　　電話：+603- 9057-8822　　傳真：+603- 9057-6622
　　　　　　Email：cite@cite.com.my
印　　　刷／禹利電子分色有限公司
初　　　版／2024 年 3 月
定　　　價／600 元
I S B N　978-626-7431-21-4
EISBN　978-626-7431-22-1（EPUB）

二〇二四年五月　慈濟大愛人文中心・紐約

城邦讀書花園
www.cite.com.tw

布克文化

「根繫何處──慈濟國際難民援助特展」的舉辦以及這本展覽紀念冊的出版,雖然在全球難民這浩大的公共議題中,如滄海一粟、微光螢火一樣渺小,但願我們此刻的行動能觸發更廣大的愛與善的漣漪。感恩為此做出貢獻的每一個人。

──慈濟大愛人文中心

在飽受戰爭蹂躪的敘利亞西北部,一名失去家園的婦女正在野地上採摘季節性農作物。照片:土耳其「世界醫師聯盟」提供

土耳其伊斯坦堡省烏克蘭難民關懷，2022

俄烏戰爭導致烏克蘭居民流離失所，慈濟展開人道援助行動，馳援烏國難民。目前在土國約有四萬名烏克蘭難民，慈濟志工透過烏克蘭協會 (Ukraine Association) 得知，部分難民家庭急需協助，3月21日慈濟人進行訪視關懷，實際了解難民處境，以評估未來援助行動，並送上物資卡給烏克蘭難民，緩解困境。攝影：Mohammed Nimr Al Jamal

約旦慈濟人援助伊拉克難民，2003

慈濟人關懷因伊拉克戰亂逃難到約旦的
伊拉克難民小朋友。照片：陳秋華提供

愛是希望

愛的能量，

是維繫天下平安的希望。

——證嚴上人靜思語

推薦序

顏博文（濟臨）

佛教慈濟慈善基金會執行長

慈濟波蘭奧坡雷家暴庇護所關懷，2023

復活節前夕，波蘭奧坡雷慈濟志工準備了毛毯、文具和復活節巧克力，前往收容受家暴婦女和兒童的「Szansa」家暴庇護所關懷。非常有經驗的社會局長毛高霞(Malgosia，右跪坐者)也陪同前來，並向孩子們介紹來自臺灣的慈濟，也向他們解說慈濟的環保毛毯是如何製作而成。照片：陳惠如提供

前不久，位於紐約的慈濟大愛人文中心（Tzu Chi Center）舉辦了「根繫何處：流離失所後的慈悲共渡」——慈濟國際難民援助特展。這不是普通的文獻展，於當下意義非同尋常。非常感謝美國慈濟團隊為之所做的一切努力，相信此次展覽也將為大愛人文中心開啟更多展覽的契機。我表心祝賀這本紀念冊的出版，撼人心魄的圖片和文字將告訴人們，遠離戰爭帶來的苦難與不幸，呼喚世界的和平與安寧。

在全球範圍內，COVID-19大流行使貧困人口的狀況愈加嚴重，俄羅斯和烏克蘭戰爭的爆發不僅加劇了全球通貨膨脹、糧食和能源危機，更使全球被迫流離失所者總數超過一億。衝突爆發時，來自十二個國家的慈濟志工在證嚴上人的慈悲指引下，齊聚波蘭，援助烏克蘭難民。通過與十一個國際和國內非政府組織協同合作，慈濟的人道救援已含括了烏克蘭及鄰近八個國家的難民。援助方式包括發放購物卡、現金卡、禦寒物資、藥品，同時還提供了醫療保健服務、語言教學、兒童教育、心理和法律諮詢以及對個人和家庭的經濟支持。這些援助一直持續至今，從未間斷。此外，一些曾在波蘭淪為難民的志工也已回到烏克蘭，決心將慈濟的援助和人道關懷帶回故鄉。

土耳其會務關懷行，2023

慈濟基金會執行長顏博文率團隊至土耳其，關心會務發展。團隊來到土耳其慈濟承租的倉庫，目前存放了10,900條支援難民的毛毯和事務用品。攝影：周利貞

在土耳其，慈濟志工胡光中、周如意和余自成為敘利亞難民援助工作奠定了堅實的基礎。二〇一五年，在他們奔走下，慈濟獲准創辦滿納海國際學校，為被迫在工廠打工的敘利亞難民兒童提供教育機會。八年之後，二〇二三年土耳其大地震，這些受助的敘利亞兒童，很多轉變成為了慈濟的青年志工。他們記、通知、身分驗證到發放，這個系統使慈濟能夠為大地震的倖存者提供快速、暢通的援助，真實地體現了一個善的循環。

二〇二三年七月，我前往土耳其，親眼目睹了佛教慈濟慈善基金會與伊斯坦堡穆斯林民眾的慈悲共渡。我們共同為土耳其的敘利亞難民兒童提供教育服務，讓幼小的心靈看到未來和希望。我期盼慈濟滿納海國際學校新校區的建設能夠早日竣工，讓更多的學生改善他們的學習與生活。

同樣，在馬來西亞、泰國、美國，慈濟志工不分國籍、政治、宗教，共同關愛當地難民。面對逆境，他們懷著無私的愛和無畏的精神，向難民伸出援手，幫助難民重建教育和生計。

最後，我想強調的是，近年來，地緣政治緊張和國家間的權力鬥爭使全球局勢日益脆弱。證嚴上人常祈求「人心淨化，社會祥和，天下無災」，而這一切的關鍵正是人類的思想意識。我們希望這本出版物能讓更多人明白和看到，無論所在何地，只有人人覺醒互助、互愛、共善，才能實現世界和諧、全球永續發展，以此開創人類的美好未來。

推薦序

塞爾維亞敘利亞難民關懷，2016

塞爾維亞是敘利亞等國難民前往歐洲的必經之
路，歐洲等十多個國家的慈濟人前往塞國關懷難
民。難民孩童舉著「We are Humans, We need go
(我是人，我要離開)」的紙板。攝影：余自成

一名來自敘利亞的難民婦女在收到援助包後帶著兩個孩子返回帳篷。土耳其伊茲密爾托爾巴勒區。照片：土耳其「世界醫師聯盟」提供

為和平努力

世間宗教都有共同的善念，

只要相勉付出愛，

自然能合和互協，

共同為世界和平而努力。

——證嚴上人靜思語

國際

合作共善

Global Partners

展現團結的力量──

深入探討全球聯盟、跨宗教合作以及佛教慈濟慈善基金會在國際賑災管理中的角色

黃恩婷（靜恩）

慈濟全球合作事務發展室主任

佛教慈濟慈善基金會與聯合國兒童基金會簽署合作備忘錄

2022年4月22日，慈濟基金會與聯合國兒童基金會(UNICEF)透過視訊簽署合作備忘錄，為受到俄烏戰事影響的兒童及其家庭提供急需的保護和服務。簽約儀式由慈濟基金會執行長顏博文、聯合國兒童基金會美國辦事處執行長麥可‧尼恩惠斯(Michael Nyenhuis，右上)，與在波蘭的慈濟美國總會執行長曾慈慧(左下前)、土耳其慈濟志工胡光中(左下右)、周如意(左下中)，及美國聯合國兒童基金會全球事業夥伴關係助理主任朱冠豪(Austin Chu，右下)透過視訊一同參與。照片：慈濟基金會提供

當今世界正面臨越來越頻繁的災難性事件，這凸顯了與宗教信仰組織建立全球合作關係的重要性。這些合作夥伴憑藉著其廣泛的網絡和資源，可以快速有效地緊急動員與提供援助。佛教慈濟慈善基金會是國際賑災中最具顯著管理成效的組織之一，一向強調跨宗教合作在危急救濟行動中的重要性。

慈濟基金會植根於佛教教義，展示了宗教信仰組織如何在救援行動中起到的重大作用，不僅為需要被救助的人們提供物質援助以及心理和精神方面的慰藉，同時還致力於展開跨宗教間的合作，這正是慈濟基金會獨樹一格的實踐法則。透過認同及尊重不同宗教之間的共通理念，慈濟基金會積極尋求與不同信仰的組織建立夥伴關係，力求帶來可執行的援助方案。

這種不同宗教間的合作可以在處理危機時擴大影響範圍，並提供更多樣化的有效資源。慈濟基金會的救災行動，尤其是其跨宗教合作，凸顯了宗教組織在全球合作共善中的潛力。他們的協作強調了將相關組織共同納入更廣泛的救災策略的必要性，同時也彼此認同各自所擁有的獨特地位和貢獻。

波蘭華沙烏克蘭難民關懷，2022

慈濟在波蘭援助烏克蘭難民，逐漸轉入中長期慈善關懷。志工們啟動慈善訪視，關懷需要幫助的烏克蘭家庭。另外有一項很重要的是孩童品格教育，陪伴烏克蘭學齡前兒童。照片：慈濟基金會提供

二〇二二年四月，慈濟基金會與天主教靈醫會國際醫療暨災難服務委員會（CADIS）簽署了一項承諾，共同在波蘭和烏克蘭開展行動，向烏克蘭難民提供援助。這些援助包括了提供生活必需品、食物、醫療服務、臨時住房和心理諮詢等，該合作計畫在五個月內幫助超過四萬人。在簽約儀式的視訊會議裡，天主教靈醫會國際醫療暨災難服務委員會的代表與靜思精舍（慈濟總部）的法師，與來自臺灣、波蘭、羅馬的與會者，共同祈禱戰爭平息，並希望世界無災無難。

慈濟對難民的援助包括了生活必需品、食物、醫療服務、臨時住房和心理諮詢，積極幫助了個人和家庭在經歷戰爭的破壞性影響和流離失所後重建生活。同時，向烏克蘭的醫療機構和摩爾多瓦共和國的難民收容社區所提供的醫療用品，無疑地對於解決受衝突影響的難民的直接健康需求至關重要。

二〇二二年五月，慈濟基金會承諾向聯合國兒童基金會的急難救助項目捐款一千萬美元，以幫助受持續戰爭影響的烏克蘭弱勢兒童和家庭；而這只是其中一個別具意義的案例，能為這些兒童和家庭提供重要的安全保護，包括無人陪伴兒童的身分識別、心理撫慰以及避免他們受到性剝削和虐待等傷害。除了支持聯合國兒童基金會外，慈濟基金會還為波蘭三個城市的難民家庭，提供了各項緊急物資以及心理和情緒的照護與關懷。

透過確保難民能實質獲得醫療服務和物資，慈濟基金會與合作夥伴一直致力於幫助減輕難民的痛苦並改善整體生活的品質。

慈濟基金會與空運連結賑災物流基金會（Airlink）、基督復臨安息日會安澤國際救援協會（ADRA International）、世界健康基金會（Project HOPE）和世界希望國際基金會（World Hope International）等非政府組織之間建立合作夥伴關係，為國際救援組織的共同合作並執行共同的目標，樹立了光輝的典範。

在二○二二年六月二日的合作備忘錄簽署儀式上，空運連結賑災物流基金會總裁兼首席執行官史蒂文·史密斯（Steven J. Smith）說：「要對如此大規模的人類苦難做出有意義的回應，需要來自多個領域的協同努力，包括公共、私營和慈善組織，利用各自的技能、專業知識和資源為烏克蘭人民帶來援助和希望。我非常高興空運連結賑災物流基金會與合作夥伴基督復臨安息日會安澤國際救援協會、世界健康基金會、世界希望國際基金會和慈濟基金會將在這個重要的聯盟中共同努力，來應對難民的人道主義需求。」

慈濟基金會執行長顏博文先生補充說：「慈濟基金會意識到這場人道危機需要很多團隊的共同努力，以確保受災難的人們得到慈悲、感恩、尊重和愛的需求與對待。我們很高興與各國際組織合作，為流離失所的烏克蘭人提供必需品和醫療用品。」

透過共同努力，慈濟基金會和非政府組織聯盟可以盡其所能地團隊合作，為受戰亂衝突影響的烏克蘭弱勢群體提供急需的援助和支持。他們致力於為重建新生活的人帶來積極及正向的影響，除了能鼓舞人心，也值得讚揚。未來，我們將會繼續面臨許多全球性的挑戰，這類跨宗教的合作夥伴關係，將為我們帶來並建立一個更美好、更慈悲與愛的世界。

佛教慈濟慈善基金會結合四個國際組織簽署合作備忘錄，提供人道援助關懷烏克蘭難民

2022年6月2日慈濟基金會與四個國際組織透過線上簽署合作備忘錄，包含空運連結賑災物流基金會(Airlink)、基督復臨安息日會安澤國際救援協會(Adventist Development and Relief Agency，簡稱ADRA)、世界健康基金會(Project Hope)、世界希望國際基金會(World Hope International)，共同為烏克蘭難民提供急需的藥物、醫療設備及其它必需品並運輸物資。由慈濟基金會執行長顏博文(第二排左視窗中)、世界希望國際基金會董事長及執行長約翰·里昂(John Lyon，第二排中)、世界健康基金會執行副總克里斯·斯科佩克(Chris Skopec，第二排右)、ADRA專案副總伊馬德·馬達納特(Imad Madanat，第三排左)、Airlink董事長及執行長史蒂文·史密斯(Steven J. Smith，第三排右)代表簽訂。照片：慈濟基金會提供

上圖：波蘭華沙烏克蘭難民關懷，2022

波蘭婦女基金會與慈濟共同成立的活動中心於6月29日開幕啟用，並於6月5日先進行對外啟用說明會。入口處，大大的告示牌上清楚地寫著：歡迎烏克蘭朋友的到來。攝影：呂嘉嘉

下圖：波蘭盧布林烏克蘭難民援助行動，2022

4月1日，慈濟捐贈1,500個睡袋給波蘭盧布林的紅十字會，協助在盧布林收容的烏克蘭難民。志工盧卡斯(Lukasz Baranowski，左三)、陳樹微(左二)、哈迪(Hady Souki，左一)與紅十字會人員進行討論。攝影：張淑兒

為援助逃離烏克蘭戰爭的難民，波蘭婦女基
金會與慈濟基金會合力運作「安全避風港」
計畫。當家長參與課程時，「安全避風港」
也為孩子準備多種活動，讓他們感到安全。
照片：慈濟波蘭志工提供

摩爾多瓦烏克蘭難民援助行動，2022

摩爾多瓦與烏克蘭相連，俄烏戰事發生後，大量難民湧入，慈濟透過合作機構以色列國際人道救援組織(IsraAID)，在當地提供難民援助服務。5月24日，慈濟聯合國團隊實際前往摩爾多瓦，拜訪以色列人道救援組織的太陽花難民心理輔導中心。美國總會執行長曾慈慧(右立者)陪伴較大的孩子學習毛線手工藝。攝影：Héctor Muniente

後頁：波蘭奧坡雷烏克蘭難民關懷，2022

上圖：慈濟在波蘭與奧坡雷企業家夫婦及奧坡雷政府三方合作共善，於7月26至29日於奧坡雷體育館(Opole Stegu Arena)進行現值卡與慈濟環保毛毯發放，援助當地的烏克蘭難民。照片：陳樹微提供

後頁：波蘭華沙烏克蘭難民關懷，2022

中圖：5月27、28日，慈濟志工在華沙的慈幼會教堂舉辦現值卡及環保毛毯發放。15歲的烏克蘭青年志工麗娜(Lina，左)協助志工分類竹筒裡複雜的硬幣。攝影：林美鳳

後頁：波蘭沃米安基烏克蘭難民關懷，2022

下圖：慈濟在波蘭援助烏克蘭難民的中長期行動中，有一項很重要的是孩童的品格教育，慈濟華沙團隊利用每個星期二和四前往合作夥伴靈醫會位於沃米安基的難民收容中心，帶動難民小朋友的品格教育課程。志工林美鳳陪伴小朋友專注投入遊戲。照片：波蘭慈濟志工提供

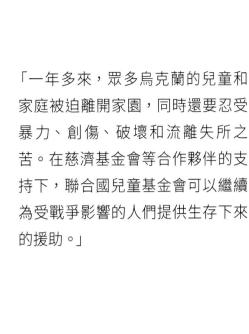

「一年多來，眾多烏克蘭的兒童和家庭被迫離開家園，同時還要忍受暴力、創傷、破壞和流離失所之苦。在慈濟基金會等合作夥伴的支持下，聯合國兒童基金會可以繼續為受戰爭影響的人們提供生存下來的援助。」

麥可・尼恩惠斯
(Michael J. Nyenhuis)
聯合國兒童基金會 (UNICEF)
美國分會執行長

「慈濟一直是以色列人道救援組織重要的合作夥伴，我在世界各地的許多賑災場合遇到慈濟，如今，我們正在烏克蘭、摩爾多瓦和羅馬尼亞合作，為數十萬人提供即時救援物資和心理援助。」

約坦・波利澤
(Yotam Polizer)
以色列人道救援組織
(IsraAID) 全球執行長

「這是一場不容低估其規模的危機！而不僅僅是規模，這場危機發展的速度，更為烏克蘭衛生系統和一線醫護人員帶來了巨大的負擔。支持世界各地的一線醫護人員，是世界健康基金會的使命。感恩此時，我們各方在此攜手，共同來執行這項至關重要而急迫的工作。」

克里斯・斯科佩克
(Chris Skopec)
世界健康基金會
(Project Hope) 執行副總裁

國際合作共善

「佛陀的慈悲和上帝的愛，都是為了拯救受苦的人們而存在，我們的基本價值觀是共通的。為了正在經歷困難的烏克蘭人，我們必須面對並共同合作。我們的責任和使命都極其重大，我們希望懷著感恩、尊重、愛向烏克蘭難民提供協助。」

荷西・伊格納西奧
(Br. José Ignacio Santaolla Saez)
天主教靈醫會國際醫療暨災難服務委員會 (Camillian Disaster Service International) 主席

「在生活中，共同的生存威脅不斷地讓我們產生隔閡，但在災難時期，我們發現這些力量卻將我們團結在一起。這讓我對人類充滿希望，希望像我們這樣的人能夠團結起來，找到比單靠個體力量更具影響力的解決方案。」

約翰・里昂
(John Lyon)
世界希望國際基金會
(World Hope International)
董事長及執行長

「透過與各組織的合作，我們齊心協力為彼此提供資源和力量，由此我們能夠共同產生更大的影響力。通常在緊急情況下，我們會解決即刻的生存的需求，即食物、水、住所等支援。然而有時因為資源和後勤的複雜性，我們忽略了對醫療用品的需求。由此我們非常感謝這種合作夥伴關係的建立，因為它是非常必要的。」

伊瑪德・馬達納特
(Imad Madanat)
基督復臨安息日會安澤國際救援協會
(Adventist Development and Relief Agency) 專案副總裁

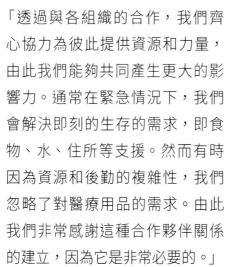

合作的力量：空運連結賑災物流基金會（Airlink）與佛教慈濟慈善基金會

史蒂文・史密斯（Steven J. Smith）

「空運連結賑災物流基金會」董事長及執行長

波蘭斯塞新烏克蘭難民援助行動，2022

波蘭斯塞新慈濟團隊與民間團體歐坦那斯基金會(Oktan-Us)合作，由慈濟捐贈物資給歐坦那斯基金會援助烏克蘭難民；圖為6月25日，發放物資運抵歐坦那斯基金會。攝影：王素真

佛教慈濟慈善基金會一直以來都是Airlink最寶貴的合作夥伴。

在過去兩年的時間裡，我們共同努力，為成千上萬受自然災害和其他危機影響的人們帶來人道援助，並讓其生活得到顯著的改善。身為Airlink的董事長兼執行長，我非常感謝能獲得慈濟基金會的支持，感謝你們的啟發、行動力以及所有敬業的員工和志工。

Airlink的使命旨在幫助受到災害和其他人道危機影響的社區；為此，我們為非政府組織提供免費的航空運輸，運送其專業救援人員和人道物資。我們認為，運輸成本和其他物流的困難不應妨礙非政府組織合作夥伴應對危機，希望為世界上最弱勢的群體提供維續生存的救助。我們與慈濟基金會有著共同的理念，並感謝慈濟與Airlink展開合作，快速有效地解決世界上遭遇災難人們的人道需求。

然而，物流在幫助難民和社區災後復原這一方面所扮演的角色往往被忽略。平均來說，供應鏈的管理成本，約佔任何人道主義專案成本的百分之七十三左右。其中，運輸是該過程中成本最高且波動最大的部分之一。慈濟對物流在人道救援時重要性的理解與關鍵性支持，對我們提供的各項援助工作極為重要。

摩爾多瓦烏克蘭難民援助行動，2022

慈濟透過合作機構以色列國際人道救援組織(IsraAID)，為在摩爾多瓦的烏克蘭難民提供援助。
5月23日，慈濟聯合國團隊實際前往摩爾多瓦拜訪合作機構與關懷難民。圖為摩爾多瓦首都基
希涅夫的雕像景觀。照片：慈濟美國總會提供

二○二二年春季，我們發起了最大規模的人道救援行動，以支持受俄烏戰爭影響的難民社區。在慈濟基金會的大力支持下，Airlink充分發揮信譽良好、經驗豐富的非政府組織合作夥伴的能力，為受戰事衝突影響的烏克蘭人，以及在摩爾多瓦、波蘭、匈牙利、斯洛伐克和羅馬尼亞尋求安全的難民，提供救生醫療用品、衛生用品和持久的醫療設備。這次援助的成果極為顯著：七十多個醫療中心獲得了醫療保健用品和藥品；行動醫療隊為烏克蘭東部無法獲得幫助的難民提供了基礎醫療保障；難民獲得了食物和其他生活必需品的支援，將近一百萬人次通過這次合作得到了救助。

Airlink也為慈濟的救援工作提供了支持，無償提供慈濟超過四十八萬美元的運輸和物流服務，協助慈濟應對烏克蘭戰爭和巴基斯坦洪災的救援工作。

Airlink與慈濟基金會之間的良好合作為許多難民社區提供了持續性的援助，支持難民重建生活——這對被救助的社區所產生的正面影響是不可低估的。我們衷心感謝慈濟基金會的支持，並期待在二○二三年及未來加強並繼續彼此的合作。

Airlink與佛教慈濟慈善基金會合作共善：

透過以合作網絡為基礎的夥伴關係模式，Airlink能更大程度地提供援助與協調，減少機構之間由於分散、未連結而造成浪費和重複工作。慈濟基金會在Airlink為受戰爭影響的烏克蘭人提供援助中起了關鍵性的貢獻。

摩爾多瓦和烏克蘭：

在慈濟基金會的三百萬美元的補助下，Airlink領導並協調了一個由非政府組織組成的聯盟，並為烏克蘭、波蘭、匈牙利、摩爾多瓦、羅馬尼亞和斯洛伐克需要醫療保健和其他援助的烏克蘭難民提供救援資金。其中，特別值得關注的是向在摩爾多瓦的烏克蘭人提供醫療援助；當時摩爾多瓦收容的難民人均數比其他國家都多，儘管摩爾多瓦人民慷慨解囊，但這仍為該國的醫療保健系統帶來了巨大壓力，甚至接近崩潰邊緣。

透過合作，Airlink與非政府組織合作夥伴聯盟成員基督復臨安息日會安澤國際救援協會（ADRA）、世界健康基金會（Project Hope）和世界希望國際基金會（World Hope International），為收治烏克蘭難民的診所提供了重要援助。該專案於二○二二年十二月完成，重點實現三個目標：

一、提供急需的藥品、醫療設備和用品，以治療因戰爭衝突引起的相關創傷，並提供與慢性病、基礎保健和傳染病有關的醫療保健。

二、強化烏克蘭和摩爾多瓦負擔過重且資源不足的衛生系統。

三、透過協調民間團體、地方市政單位與捐助者，減少運輸和物流的阻礙，增加可用於支持就地避難者、烏克蘭境內流失所者和摩爾多瓦難民的援助範圍、數量。這個聯盟確保的是能夠優先提供物資及援助給最緊急的項目或單位，以支持仍面臨

巨大壓力的衛生系統。

該計畫以供應鏈管理和物流為核心，為受戰事衝突影響的烏克蘭人以及在摩爾多瓦和羅馬尼亞尋求安全庇護的難民提供健康急需的醫療用品、衛生用品和穩定醫療設備。該聯盟總共向當地七十多個醫療機構和組織運送了五十一萬四千九百零七磅的援助物資，直接幫助了數十萬人。

事實證明，與慈濟基金會的合作對非政府組織來說非常成功且具非凡價值，因此，另外四個非營利組織也加入了該聯盟，並從這項合作中受益。Airlink團隊和我們的非政府組織合作夥伴非常感謝慈濟基金會的遠見，他們為這次的項目提供啟動資金，並在運作過程中展現了彈性與靈活性，使項目得到擴展。Airlink的非營利合作夥伴也透過該項目節省了超過七十七萬四千美元的運輸成本。

二○二二年巴基斯坦洪災：

二○二二年，巴基斯坦經歷了有史以來最嚴重的洪水災害。據估計，該國三分之一的地區被淹沒，超過三千三百萬人受到影響。當時聯合國估計，近百萬棟房屋遭到破壞，超過七十萬頭牲畜死亡，二百萬英畝的農作物被毀。

在信德省（Sindh）和俾路支（Balochistan）省，難民們沒有合適的避難所，只能住在路邊自己搭建的營地裡。隨著十二月冬季的逼近，慈濟基金會希望發放慈濟環保毛毯，為受洪水影

響的人們提供溫暖和支持來度過寒冷的冬季。

在Airlink的協助下，由合作夥伴卡達航空和Skyways來運輸救災物資，慈濟基金會及時解決了洪水受災民眾的燃眉之急，為一萬零四百一十六個家庭提供了一萬六千六百零八條毛毯。

Airlink與慈濟合作提供了不須轉手其他管道的直接運輸支持，在物資原始提供地提取救援物資到將這些物資運送到目的地的指定倉庫，Airlink協調了包括物流、運輸和清關等所有程序，因此救援組織可以專注於規劃如何發放而不必擔心運輸配送。

特別值得一提的是，受影響地區位於巴基斯坦一處沒有慈濟分會和志工的區域，這增加了援助發送過程的複雜性，尤其是在清關方面。；Airlink提供了清關協助，由其在巴基斯坦的合作清關代理機構幫助救援物資順利通行。

Airlink協調所有運輸流程，使慈濟能夠將精力和時間專注於與當地非政府組織合作、規劃如何發放物資；這些組織包括We Care基金會、伊斯蘭救濟組織、Shirkat Gah婦女資源中心、麥地那伊斯蘭研究中心（MIRC）和天主教靈醫會國際醫療暨災難服務委員會（CADIS），共同向三萬一千個家庭分發食品和物資。

巴基斯坦水患關懷發放，2022

巴基斯坦世紀洪災，慈濟與伊斯蘭援助(Islamic Relief)慈善組織合作，在災區進行物資發放。圖為伊斯蘭援助慈善組織於信德省(Sindh)進行發放糧食包、淨水劑及蚊帳。工作人員進行身分確認與發放名單進行交叉核對。照片：慈濟宗教處提供

約旦札塔里（Za'atari）難民營營外帳篷區關懷，2016

住在札塔里難民營營外帳篷區的小女孩，穿著慈濟志工贈送的嶄新外套，與身後的「家」形成強烈對比；簡陋的帳篷無法抵擋寒風，每個月的租金仍要四十元約幣。攝影：黃筱哲

讓我們並肩療癒：一場流離失所後的慈悲之旅

阿里斯特洛·米蘭達神父
天主教靈醫會國際醫療暨災難服務委員會執行董事

能在慈濟這場意義非凡的全球難民援助特展中分享一些心得，我感到既榮幸又卑微。面對流離失所的人們，用一份慈悲心與他們並肩同行，具有深遠的影響。我也很感激能有這樣的機會，以天主教靈醫會國際醫療暨災難服務委員會（Camillian Disaster Service International，簡稱CADIS）主任的身分，來分享我們在「根繫何處：流離失所後的慈悲共渡」這一主題展覽中的故事。在與慈濟合作的旅程裡，我們攜手並肩，在全球為那些流離失所的人們和社區，播下希望和療癒的種子。

天主教靈醫會國際醫療暨災難服務委員會（CADIS）於二○一六年在義大利羅馬成立，是一個由卡米利安會（The Camilian）國際人道主義基金會支持的非營利組織。「卡米利安會」是一個天主教會，由一位皈依的傭兵聖卡米盧斯·德·萊利斯（Saint Camillus de Lellis）於一五八六年創立，其成員在全球四十二個國家開展醫療保健服務，是病人、護理人員、醫院的守護神。許多成員因照顧流行病病患以及戰爭中的傷者而往生，用行動詮釋了醫者仁心的願力與堅持。

二○二○年COVID-19最嚴重的時候，透過CADIS的一個組織「印度卡米利安工作小組」（CTF），CADIS與慈濟在印度開始了首次合作，為十三個邦的八百五十四個村莊超過五十三萬人提供物資援助和心靈支持。此一因緣，成就了雙方在後續面對烏克蘭難民的困境時，繼續合作並開花結果。我們團結一致，為難民們帶去了細緻而有成效的關懷與幫助。

佛教慈濟慈善基金會與天主教靈醫會國際醫療暨災難服務委員會簽署合作備忘錄

2022年4月30日，為擴大對烏克蘭難民的援助，慈濟基金會與天主教靈醫會國際醫療暨災難服務委員會(Camillian Disaster Service International)簽署合作備忘錄，預計共同在波蘭、烏克蘭投入包含提供食品和必需品、現值卡、醫療服務、安置收容所、心理與技能輔導等人道援助。簽約儀式中，由天主教靈醫會國際醫療暨災難服務委員會主席荷西‧伊格納西奧(Br. José Ignacio Santaolalla Saez，左視窗中)、執行董事阿里斯特洛神父(Fr. Aristelo Miranda, MI，左視窗右)與慈濟基金會執行長顏博文(右視窗中)代表簽約。照片：慈濟花蓮本會提供

二○二二年五月，CADIS和慈濟依據烏克蘭難民的需求，採取了更機動和有方向性的援助措施。迄今為止，已向超過三十萬烏克蘭難民提供了救濟（食物、非食物、心理支持）和重建援助（工作、住所、醫療保健）。我們雙方的合作基於慈善、同理心、尊重、人性尊嚴並跨越宗教信仰，在彼此共同價值觀的啟發中，展現各自獨特的能力和信念。

當今的世界就像一個地球村，來自不同宗教、傳統的人們時常毗鄰共存，因而，建立有著共同宗旨，以及對人性和心靈渴望的橋梁，變得更為重要。CADIS和慈濟都堅信跨宗教合作具有強大的力量，儘管我們在信仰、儀規和行事作法上存在一定的差異，但共同的價值觀和追求，是彼此攜手前行的基礎，為世界受災難影響的社區帶來正向的力量是一致的目標。我們對影響社區的常見生存和環境問題，如貧窮、飢餓、無家可歸、氣候變化和各種歧視、不平等等達成人道主義上的共識，針對這些共同關心的問題相互凝聚共識，形成獨特的優勢和視角去解決問題，並透過不同的項目來理解彼此的價值觀、道德規範和行動原則。因此，我們團結且富同理心的合作，持續向更多的組織與人們釋放出強烈的訊號——不同信仰的人們可以為了更大的善而走到一起。

當前世界，各種衝突、環境劇變和社會經濟不平等的因素，如狂風般將人性和夢想連根拔起，而CADIS和慈濟像燈塔一樣堅定地屹立著。我們彼此承諾為減輕那些流離失所者的痛苦而共同努力，體現了人類應有的堅韌和慈悲的本懷。在探索「根繫何處：流離失所後的慈悲共渡」這個展覽中所捕捉到的瞬間時，那些曾在混亂中充滿勇氣、團結和轉機的故事又一一展現在我們眼前。這是一個令人充滿希望的標誌，為我們努力去改變複雜世界賦予了意義。

國際合作共善

展覽中的圖像不只是一幅幅展品，它們富含人類豐富多樣的經驗更提醒著我們，即使在流離失所的深淵中，個體的重生和轉變的能力也是無限的。站在圖像前，我們被鼓舞著應要有所行動，希望能為那些被迫離開家園、四處漂泊的人們，給予支持並為他們合作、付出，盡一己之力。人們來到這個展覽時，這些影像會點燃我們心中慈悲的火焰，激勵我們加入這場大愛行動，一起去療癒傷者的傷口，並讓他們能夠提振精神和重建生活。

當我們凝視展覽中那些喚人深省的照片和影像時，讓我們一起展望未來，慈悲的種子將會繼續結出愛與善的果實。我們同行的旅程並未就此結束，還有更多的可能性在等著我們。CADIS和慈濟有著共同的願景：不讓任何人在流離失所的風暴中漂泊，讓慈悲成為我們共通的語言，懷著無國界的愛隨時伸出援助之手。

感謝這個展覽所開啟的一段慈悲之旅——攜手並肩，讓我們一起為不得不背井離鄉的人們鋪平一條治癒和希望之路，並為他們開啟未來之路。；在那裡，每個人的心靈都能得到慰藉、支持，並找到新的家。CADIS仍將致力於團結合作，一起提供有效的難民救助和協助重建；透過共同努力，我們可以真正改變世界各地難民的生活，並協助尋找後續解決方案的方法。我們呼籲每個人為這個複雜但崇高的使命來付出與貢獻己能，陪伴難民們到達一個可以稱之為「家」的地方。

我想用一句著名的非洲諺語來總結我的回顧：「如果你想走得快，就一個人行動；如果你想走得遠，讓大家一起攜手前行。」攜手並肩，我們可以幫助難民重建生活。雖然在短期內，僅僅依靠個體的努力和資源似乎會有一定的效果，但如果與他人建立團隊成為合作夥伴，卻可以讓我們克服各種困難，不斷推進。儘管可能會慢一些，但終將讓我們能走得更遠。這樣的結果是：所有難民依舊能在黑暗中保持他們的信念與尊嚴，安然地生活。這是一場有著相同目的地和堅定信心的奉獻之旅，它提醒著我們，慈悲與同理心是無限量的，人心的凝聚是比分歧更強大的力量。讓我們攜手努力建造一個以慈悲和同理心為基石的世界——再沒有人漂泊無助，因為我們並肩站在一起。

我想用一句著名的非洲諺語來總結我的回顧：「如果你想走得快，就一個人行動；如果你想走得更遠，讓大家一起攜手前行。」

上圖：波蘭克拉科夫烏克蘭難民援助行動，2022

5月21日，慈濟聯合國團隊前往波蘭克拉科夫拜訪天主教靈醫會的醫療服務中心，了解美國慈濟人醫會與靈醫會在克拉科夫辦理難民義診的可能性及地點。醫療服務中心旁的靈醫會教堂已經115年，非常具有歷史價值。照片：慈濟美國總會提供

右圖：印度COVID-19疫情物資發放，2021

COVID-19疫情肆虐印度，慈濟基金會結合印度天主教靈醫會(ST. CAMILLIANS PROVINCE - INDIA)以及所屬的慈善機構Sneha Charitable Trust展開跨宗教合作，為貧困家庭發放糧食，讓他們有充足的食物度過難關。在德里貧民區發放，需要顧及安全及預防搶糧事件發生，為此，靈醫會結合當地20個宗教及婦女協會，走入貧區進行物資發放。照片：印度天主教靈醫會提供

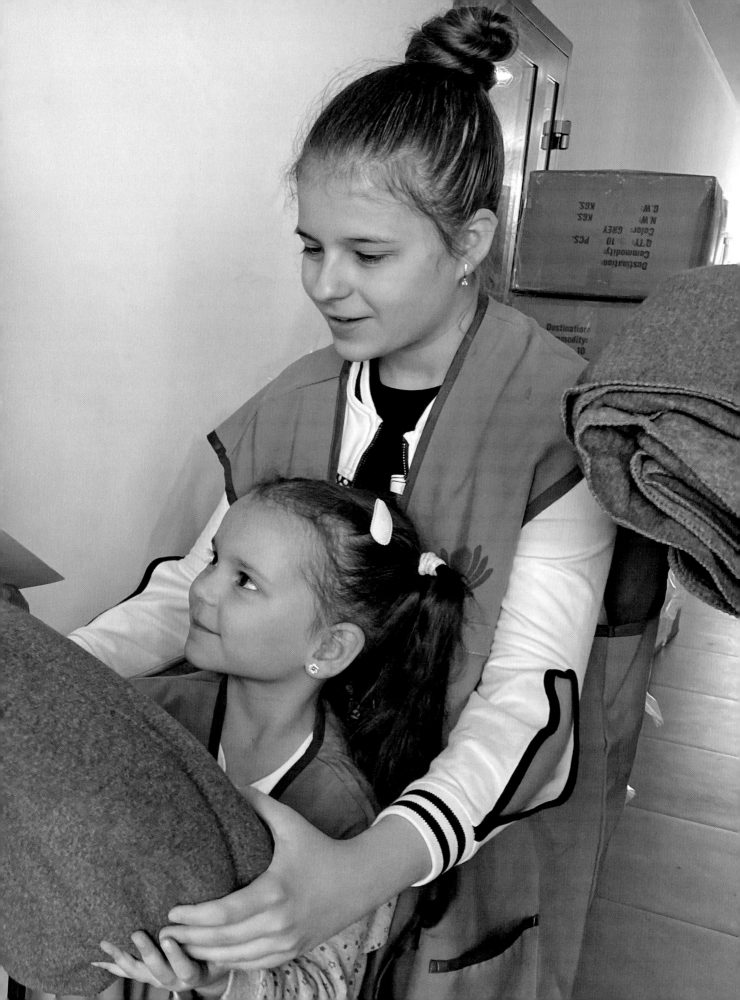

波蘭波茲南烏克蘭難民關懷，2022

6月5日，波蘭波茲南慈濟團隊在羅基尼察區
(Rokietnica)消防局的附屬會議廳進行發放，發
放名單來自四個政府單位。發放毛毯區由慈濟小
志工負責，小志工雙手奉上毛毯並說感恩，可愛
的模樣讓大家帶著微笑離開。攝影：呂佩玲

相信、發願、行動

志工菩薩無私付出，時時關懷照顧眾生，

累積「信、願、行」——相信、發願、行動，

一旦災難發生，

就如菩薩從地湧出，

為人世間投入付出。

——證嚴上人靜思語

慈濟

志工

Tzu Chi Volunteers

投身難民救助，慈濟全球志工攜愛前行

黃思賢
慈濟全球志工總督導

自一九八九年四月第一次在花蓮見到證嚴上人，我深深地被證嚴上人的智慧與慈悲所震撼，此後皈依上人，得賜法號「思賢」。自此以後，我便全身心、無保留地追隨證嚴上人，投入慈濟，推動慈濟四大志業、八大法印，作證嚴上人的「腳」，哪裡需要，便二話不說，去到哪裡。

慈濟自一九九一年援助孟加拉水患，揭開國際賑災的序幕起，迄今援助一百三十三個國家地區，對於受災國家，除了提供糧食、衣被、穀種、藥品的緊急援助外，還援助建房、建校、協助開發水源、提供義診；關懷項目儘管有別，「尊重生命」理念卻是始終如一。

全球難民關懷是慈濟實踐國際急難救助中重要的一環，作為靜思弟子，深刻體會到證嚴上人所說「人傷我痛，人苦我悲」的情懷，三十多年來，我更是有福報參與到多次的國際急難救援。

上圖：阿富汗賑災，2002

慈濟與美國騎士橋國際救援組織(KBI)援助阿富汗，
馳援飽受旱災、內戰及阿富汗戰爭之苦的民眾。
圖：艾巴克市廢墟難民關懷，難民小朋友經歷風
霜，面對相機，臉上神情漠然。照片：黃思賢提供

右圖：土耳其難民關懷

敘利亞難民孩子熱情地向志工們揮手告別。照片：
土耳其「世界醫師聯盟」提供

依循「直接、重點、尊重、務實、及時」的急難救助原則，在為難民提供緊急物資支援的同時，慈濟也結合醫療、教育、人文關懷等中長期關懷計畫，幫忙災民與難民自立自強，翻轉人生，重新站起來。

無論是殘酷無情的自然災害如華東水災、毀滅性的菲律賓海燕風災、南亞海嘯、海地超強地震、土敘大地震，還是因戰爭人禍導致的人道災難如美國九一一恐怖襲擊、俄烏衝突，在這個動盪不安的世界裡，身著藍天白雲制服的慈濟志工從不缺席。

慈濟即將走入第五十八個年頭，藉此機會，也感恩過去所有參與到慈濟國際急難救助中的志工菩薩，感恩他們的無私付出，啟發了自己的愛心，也照亮了那些在幽暗中飽受苦難的生命。

二〇二三年十月七日，以色列、哈瑪斯硝煙再起。數以萬計手無寸鐵的平民遭受戰火襲擊，沒有什麼比這更讓人痛心。傳播愛與善，並積極建立一個跨越種族、宗教隔閡，可以互助互愛的橋梁，是全球慈濟志工一直堅持的行動理念，也是上人的諄諄教誨。在此，我再次呼籲我們以愛與善念來化解當下的危機，否則，衝突與災難永遠無法平息。

幸而亂世之外，有大愛永恆，慈濟如燈塔為伴，法船滿載星夢，駛向和平與愛的彼岸。

攝影：Jaime Puerta

信念與行動 必須始終一致

胡 光 中

慈濟土耳其聯絡處負責人

首位穆斯林慈濟委員

胡光中

信念與行動，必須始終一致

「世界上沒有人想成為難民，但現實是，許多人在毫無準備的情況下成為難民。這是全世界所有人的責任，來重視這個問題，讓更多的人明白：這個世界需要和平而非戰爭。」

左圖：土耳其滿納海國際學校

暮色下的伊斯坦堡省蘇丹加濟市。攝影：Hannah Whisenant

胡光中，一名穆斯林，因著「愛與善」的信念，和慈濟走在了一起；多年來克服重重困難，在土耳其無怨無悔地默默耕耘。

他是創辦土耳其滿納海國際學校（El Menahi International School）的主要推動者之一，這所學校為敘利亞難民兒童提供了急需的教育與協助。迄今為止，他的行動已經直接、積極地影響了四千多名兒童及其家庭的生活。

敘利亞人講阿拉伯語，而不是土耳其語，所以即使難民童們有經濟能力上學，他們也不太可能去土耳其本地學校上學。然而，首要的問題還是他們是否能負擔得起學費。成年難民在就業方面已然困難重重，他們往往只能從事低薪的非技術性的工作，即使他們有資格做更多的事情。更令人心碎的是，年齡小到六歲的難民兒童經常就被僱用作工廠的勞工，因為他們可以容納在較小的空間做工，工資更是驚人的低廉，且由於勞動法不適用於他們，他們因此很容易受到來自管理者的虐待。

胡光中在慈濟美國長島支會的演講中舉例分享了一個敘利亞兒童的故事。這個孩子每天輪班十三個小時，被規定不能坐著，一天只能有十三分鐘的休息時間來使用衛生間。他看上去大約十二歲，已經三年多沒有上學了；那些年，無論身體和內心，他都承受著巨大的痛苦。這些難民孩子正在經受著的苦難，胡光中感同身受。設立一所學校，幫助孩子們回歸正常的學習和生活成為了胡光中當下篤定的目標。

讓滿納海國際學校成真的過程並非一帆風順。最初，慈濟與一些學校達成協議，這些學校上午有課，下午就可以空出教室讓敘利亞難民孩子上學。然而，由於對敘利亞難民的歧視，即使孩子們並不在同時段上課，這些學校裡土耳其學生的家長表達抗議，拒絕讓難民兒童與自己的孩子使用同一間教室。抗議的家長們聯手一起封鎖學校，阻止難民學生進入學校。對於許多土耳其人來說，敘利亞難民是導致土耳其經濟變差的代罪羔羊。胡光中努力與各方協調溝通，最終，他對難民的同理心和積極行動贏得了勝利，滿納海國際學校成為了真實。

滿納海的課程包括：數學、物理、化學、歷史，還有體育課。學校使用阿拉伯語、英語和土耳其語。目前，他們正在規劃將中文和宗教研究添加到課程中，例如：古蘭經、伊斯蘭文化及其教義。

身為一名穆斯林，胡光中去到臺灣花蓮，曾向佛教慈濟慈善基金會的創始人證嚴上人匯報過多個類似的案例。讓證嚴上人印象深刻的是，即使面臨暴力或虐待，大多數敘利亞難民也極不願意報警，因為他們很害怕被驅逐出境。上人表示，如果不加以關切，這些難民，特別是兒童，將會逐漸仇恨壓迫他們的人和這個世界，最終可能轉向暴力和犯罪作為對社會的報復。她堅定認為這些難民兒童必須接受教育，這不僅能讓他們有機會過較好的生活，還能讓他們獲得安全感和尊重感。胡光中非常認同上人的觀點。

慈濟志工

胡光中並不是唯一一個致力於幫助土耳其境內敘利亞難民的人，與他一起工作的還有許多是來自敘利亞的志工，他們本身也都是難民。這些志工原本在敘利亞從事各行各業，有些就是學校裡的老師，但敘利亞內戰爆發後，他們逃離到土耳其。在難民兒童學校創辦之前，這些人在紡織廠或製鞋廠等從事非技術性的工作；學校成立後，他們來當老師，也成為了慈濟志工或是慈濟基金會的工作人員，以此來回饋慈濟給予他們的幫助。

胡光中對未來的希望是，二十或三十年後，滿納海國際學校的校友能夠記得慈濟設立了滿納海，記得慈濟給予了他們對未來的嚮往與希望。更重要的是，他希望學生們有一天能將他們所獲得的慈悲和尊重繼續傳遞下去。可喜的是，一些溫馨的行動說明了他不必等待數十年後才能看到自己苦心奔走的成果，譬如學校成立後的幾年裡，滿納海的師生們一起為慈濟其他各種救災活動點滴匯集，籌得了數百萬元新臺幣的愛心。

作為一名虔誠的穆斯林，一開始胡光中對慈濟這個佛教組織來救助非佛教徒確實曾抱有疑慮，他懷疑讓受助的人皈依佛教才是慈濟的最終目標。但與證嚴上人的第一次交談，就消除了他這個疑慮。上人告訴他，年輕獨自修行時，有時候要上山撿木柴，途中會經過一座教堂，自己總是在教堂前深深鞠躬；自己雖然不是基督徒，但對所有的基督徒都表示深深的尊重。上人

慈濟志工

還說：「當我們消除種族、國籍、語言、膚色、宗教的差異時，剩下的就只有一個字——愛。」上人曾問胡光中，伊斯蘭教的教義裡是否包括愛？他回答說，當然是，伊斯蘭教真主的眾多名字之一是al-Wadud，翻譯過來就是「大愛」。上人又問，真主的愛是否有邊界？他回答說：「不，無邊無界。」

胡光中表示，伊斯蘭教的核心理念之一是，你的信仰或信念與你的行動必須始終保持一致。如果你相信真主的愛是無邊界的，並且你在這個世界表達這種愛，那麼你必須將其付諸行動——僅有信仰是不夠的，必須有行動。同樣，慈濟的核心理念是將慈悲付諸行動；慈悲是美好的、崇高的，但如果沒有行動，又有什麼用呢？

愛可以跨越宗教種族，無邊無界。每當想到這裡，胡光中內心充滿感慨：「世界上沒有人想成為難民，但現實是，許多人在毫無準備的情況下成為了難民。這是全世界所有人的責任，來重視這個問題，讓更多的人明白：這個世界需要和平而非戰爭。」

土耳其滿納海國際學校

上圖：禱告室裡，胡光中與滿納海國際學校師生一起禱告。在很多難民孩子心裡，胡光中就是像爸爸一樣的存在。攝影：Hannah Whisenant

右頁圖：在滿納海國際學校裡，無數來自敘利亞的難民孩子實現了命運的翻轉。攝影：Hannah Whisenant

上人曾問胡光中，
伊斯蘭教的教義裡是否包括愛？
他回答說，當然是，
伊斯蘭教真主的眾多名字之一
是 al-Wadud，
翻譯過來就是「大愛」。

上人又問，真主的愛是否有邊界？
他回答說：「不，無邊無界。」

土耳其滿納海國際學校

上圖：敘利亞難民學童歡喜地在滿納海國際學校上學。攝影：范婷

右圖：滿納海，阿拉伯語裡的意思是沙漠裡的綠洲。胡光中與妻子周如意以及志工們全心投入，克服種種困難，終於為難民孩子迎來了這片教育裡的綠洲。攝影：范婷

守護綠洲上的每一朵花

周如意（慈榮）

慈濟土耳其志工

周如意

守護綠洲上的

每一朵花

「在這片土地上，我們跟
他們是同一群人，就是這
樣子生活在這片土地上，
他們難過，我們也一樣感
到了難過。」

左圖：土耳其伊斯坦堡省蘇丹加濟市敘利亞難民家訪，2014

慈濟志工訪視因戰亂逃難到土耳其的敘利亞難民，瞭解中小學學生的就學情形，造冊評估發放助學金事宜。慈濟志工胡光中(左二)與周如意(左一)填寫學生資料。攝影：余自成

前頁圖：土耳其都覺市地震關懷，1999

土耳其於1999年11月12日再次遭遇芮氏規模7以上的強震，慈濟志工緊急採購5,000條毛毯前往災區進行發放。11月15日，慈濟志工胡光中(右三)與周如意(右二)帶著兒子胡雲凱(右四)與四位留學生前來都覺災區協助毛毯發放。照片：慈濟花蓮本會提供

一九九六年，周如意與丈夫胡光中前往土耳其經商、生活，土耳其自此成為了他們夫婦倆的第二個家鄉。一九九九年八月，土耳其遭遇芮氏規模七點四的強烈大地震，夫妻二人遇見了從臺灣前來支援賑災的慈濟團隊。伊斯蘭教和佛教中對愛與善的共通信念，使胡光中與周如意積極加入了慈濟救援賑災的行列，並在之後成為了慈濟在土耳其志工行列的中堅力量。

二〇一四年，敘利亞內戰烽火再起，大量難民湧入土耳其。周如意目睹一群群在首都伊斯坦堡街頭遊蕩的敘利亞難民孩子沿街乞討，到垃圾桶裡撿東西充飢，或為了生存被迫淪為非法童工；在與志工去發放物資的時候，周如意遇見難民要拿慈濟發放的毛毯來換錢支付其孩子的學費。十五年前大地震致使災民們流離失所的悲慘情景，此時再次湧上周如意的心頭，使那雙平日裡笑起來彎如新月的眼睛噙滿淚水。她想：「在這片土地上，我們跟他們是同一群人，就是這樣子生活在這片土地上，他們難過，我們也一樣感到了難過。」周如意當時發願，希望街上乞討的敘利亞孩子，都能變成背書包上學的孩子。

願望的種子在心裡發芽生長，並化作了力量與行動。夫婦倆和另一位臺灣志工余自成及敘利亞籍志工們，在晚上挨家挨戶拜訪調查，找出失學的難民孩子，並登記資料回報慈濟。二〇一五年，土耳其全境第一所難民學校——滿納海國際學校在慈濟和社會各界的努力之下成立了。

慈濟志工

滿納海（Menahij），在阿拉伯文裡的原意是「沙漠中的綠洲」。從最初資助五百多位難民兒童上學，到如今學校能夠容納三千多位孩子們學習，這一路，周如意像一位慈母般守護著孩子們，讓他們在這片綠洲上綻放出如花朵般的笑容。

「她把我們結合起來，教我們做人的道理。她把我們當成正常的孩子，就好像我們是她的孩子一般。我們每次都是迫不及待等著跟她見面，一分鐘、一分鐘地等待，有如在充滿愛的空氣中寫一本書——寫關於她對我們所有的好。」在一封來自滿納海的學生充滿了詩意的書信裡，我們得以看見這位母親對待難民孩子真誠的心。

望著在學校裡安心學習的學生們，周如意的雙眼裡滿是欣喜和讚嘆。她明白對這些難民孩子來說，擁有一個和平美好的未來，這條路還很漫長，但她深信，教會孩子「愛」與「善」，就像是點亮任何黑暗道路的明燈。如今，這慈愛的雙眸中，更添加了一份堅定的目光。

以下為慈濟大愛人文中心（TCC）對周如意（周）的採訪整理，發表前經由受訪者審校。

土耳其伊斯坦堡省蘇丹加濟市敘利亞難民關懷，2016

土耳其境內約有兩百多萬敘利亞難民，慈濟志工長期關懷住在蘇丹加濟市的難民家庭。周如意教導小朋友手語，準備在慈濟難民義診中心的慶祝茶會中展現成果。攝影：蕭耀華

TCC：您在滿納海國際學校特別為七到十二年級學生開辦的人文課，其中包括插花和茶道。在一個為難民孩子們解決生存問題的學校裡開設這些看似「奢侈」、「浪漫」的課程，這個初衷和動力是什麼？以及學生們的反饋是怎樣的？

周：我記得第一次學插花的時候，我的老師用很簡單的三個東西便插成一盆小花，然後跟我說：「插花其實很貴的，我們都自己種花來插。」第二次是慈濟的阿利師姊在我出國的前一天傳授給我一些經驗，她說臨時教我來不及了，但是要我記得：不管我們做什麼事，最重要的目的就是「陪伴」，陪伴難民們走過這條辛苦的路。

當我回到土耳其，那時候是土耳其的政變以後，學校的政策改變了，由基金會贊助的學校都不能親自督管，改由政府管理。慈濟贊助的學校也不例外，所以我們也看不到學生。那時候慈濟在土耳其建立的義診中心地剛剛開幕，義診中心地下室就作為我們的辦公室，物資發放也在那裡，我也在那裡招收了第一批的人文課程的學生。我們天天上課，有插花、茶道還有中文課，學生雖然只有十幾位，但是都很單純。

我從教他們插花、茶道裡訓練他們的禮儀，讓他們變成非常有人文氣質的學生。還有教導手語，訓練講故事，陪伴他們到義診中心去服務病人，雖然病人看不太懂我們比手語是什麼意思，但是能感受到我們很有誠意為病人服務。

還有每個月的發放，我都會帶領著這些孩子們一起做，久而久之他們也成為了一個個很有慈濟精神的志工，看著他們幫忙擺放鞋子、洗碗、清潔，就覺得他們好有教養。後來新的滿納海國際學校成立以後，他們被分發到土耳其學校去了，所以這些人文課程又招收其他新的學生。

我後來也陸續開了一些班級繼續教導插花和茶道，除了孩子，學校的教師也會來上課。有些孩子來我班上的時候臉上是帶著笑容的，很禮貌的那種。看到我帶來的各種美麗的花朵，聞著花香，露出開心的笑容。我也放著一些風潮音樂和古箏樂曲當背景音樂，一步一步教他們插出一盆花，當他們看到自己手中光禿禿的盆子和海綿竟然在巧妙的安排下變成一盆美麗的風景，臉上展現出的燦爛笑容和剛進門時的笑容是很不一樣的，那是一種發自內心的喜悅，臉上散發著光芒，體會到幸福的感覺。

我並沒有特意去區分難民或是普通民眾，只是覺得既然有人願意學習那我就教他們，雖然土耳其「花」的價格比較貴，但是我覺得是值得的。至於茶道雖然茶費不高，但也是要用心學習，這也是一門學問和藝術。當你看到學生彬彬有禮地端著茶杯、茶食給我們或客人的時候，心裡就會讚嘆：多好的孩子呀！多麼有禮儀！這就是我們慈濟精神教出來的孩子，非常有人文素養。

另外，靜思語也是課程裡非常重要的一環，他們學習證嚴上人的話語，將這些精神潛移默化地帶入生活之中。

TCC：滿納海現在共有教師一百四十名，其中很多也是被迫逃難到土耳其的敘利亞難民。在我看來，這裡不但是三千多個流離失所的未成年孩子們的家，也為教師們提供了一個安定的就業環境。擁有相同的根與背景，他們對孩子們的遭遇著新的生命身受。在滿納海這個「社區」中，教師們也在經歷著新的生命旅程。您能向讀者介紹一下，學校是如何關懷、培育這些敘利亞籍教師的？同時可以分享一兩位教師的故事嗎？

周：滿納海國際學校在蘇丹加濟市 (Sultan Ghazi) 培育了許多敘利亞籍老師，應該說讓許多敘利亞籍老師能夠重拾做人的尊嚴，繼續教導學生。例如我們將全校最好最大的教室留給老師做休息室，外面有大理石做成的陽臺讓老師可以在外面喝咖啡、欣賞風景，因為我們相信只有感受到疼愛的老師、心裡充滿愛的老師，才能夠愛孩子，給予學生滿滿的愛。

像康天怡、馬力克老師兩位老師，經過慈濟大學兩年的培訓後也通過華語檢定考試，獲得證書。馬力克老師遇到任何機會都會使用中文來表達對慈濟的愛和感恩，我也非常感激他將所學的使用出來，讓學問轉化成價值。

滿納海國際學校的老師們都是以品格教育為優先，學歷次之；我們要求學生們也是以品格為先，學問成績次之。

TCC：在之前的採訪裡，您說您的夢想是每個孩子都可以開心地背上書包上學。也看到孩子們在給您的信中寫道：您把他們當成正常的孩子，就好像是您自己的孩子一般。這是對孩子們最好的尊重，是不一般的愛和智慧！同時，我也認為大人和孩子是相互滋養、相互學習成長。可以和我們分享幾個讓您自豪、感動，或讓您產生思考與改變的孩子的故事嗎？

周：每個孩子都有讓我感動的地方，因為每個人背後都有一個故事，只是孩子們願不願意再說起這些故事而已。我很高興能夠成為他們的中文老師，教導中文以外也讓他們瞭解慈濟的精神，還有中華文化。我現在的中文班上有一對姊妹花，姊姊的中文名字是心如，妹妹的中文名字是銀鈴，她們常常給我回饋就是說「老師我愛你」，每次看到他們的笑臉就會讓我覺得很貼心。另一個學生漢靖娜，去年讓她背靜思語，很長的一大段文字，沒想到她雖然看起來文弱但卻做到了，而且也唸得很好，讓我刮目相看，所以今年再接再厲，讓她繼續學習再難一點的句子，她也勇於挑戰，願意給自己機會更上一層樓。

還有學生馬平安、海麗，為了分擔家計，現在下課後還要去打工。但是遇到中文課時他們都會儘量來上課。從早上打工直到下午，然後繼續學習中文，另一個上完課以後還要打工，這份堅持的精神讓我很感動，覺得很窩心。

今年這些學生都通過華語檢定考試，拿到了中華民國教育部的華語檢定證書，這給予我們師生們非常大的鼓勵。他們非常

土耳其伊斯坦堡省蘇丹加濟市「滿納海國際學校」，2019

來自敘利亞的教師和工作人員得以在學校穩定工作，並能夠幫助來自相同
文化、語言和宗教背景且經歷相似的孩子。這使他們成為理想的學習榜
樣，幫助學生處理他們所經歷的創傷。攝影：Jaime Puerta

認真，現在除了阿拉伯文、土耳其文、英文以外，還多會了中文。這拓寬了他們的視野，讓他們成為世界性的公民。

TCC：您在多年的國際賑災和難民救助中，一定遇見過許多受困的女性難民，她們往往比男性面臨更嚴酷的生存挑戰，更加無力做出選擇。慈濟是如何鼓勵幫助她們的？您作為一位資深、受人愛戴的女性志工，有什麼可以分享給讀者的感想嗎？

周：是的，我聽過許多女性難民的故事，那是血和淚交織而成的故事。例如有位懷孕的婦女，帶著她先天不良的兒子逃過邊界進入土耳其。她描述道：我先跳邊界的土坑，上去了之後拖著懷孕七個月的身體把兒子再拉出來。到了伊斯坦堡他們一開始連住的地方都沒有，後來和親戚們住在一起。當她展示給我她的孩子們時，她是多麼的驕傲，我永遠不會忘記她那堅強的眼神及笑容！那是因為她把孩子們平安地送到這裡並且活了下來。作為一個母親，這是非常偉大並且韌性十足的，我以這位母親為榮。

我常常擁抱這些婦女，不管是發放的時候，家訪的時候，還是看見她們哭泣的時候，我知道溫暖的擁抱抵過千言萬語。慈濟在蘇丹加濟市每個月幫助八千戶的難民家庭，每個家都有一位竭力支撐家庭的女人，我也常常鼓勵她們：女人可以撐起半邊天。她們都很開心，感覺自己受到重視，不是孤單的人。

我很感謝慈濟給我機會幫助這些婦女和家庭，包括教她們的孩子中文，因為我的付出溫暖了他們的生命，而我也覺得很充實。靜思語說得好，「幫助別人就是幫助自己」。為了陪伴這些敘利亞鄉親我學習了茶道、花道——這些以前我從來沒學過的美好事物。即使我的經驗不及茶道、花道老師們的十分之一，但我仍然感到歡喜，盡我所能去陪伴他們，撫慰他們，直到他們走上通往心裡那個家園的路。

上圖：土耳其伊斯坦堡省蘇丹加濟市敘利亞難民關懷，2015

慈濟志工與敘利亞老師向土耳其政府申請辦學，為敘利亞難民學童成立第一所半公立的敘利亞中小學「滿納海國際學校」。圖：周如意與學生互動。攝影：余自成

右圖：土耳其南部地震救援，2023

慈濟於6月10日在滿納海國際學校舉行地震賑災發放，發放對象為上個場次錯過的土耳其及敘利亞籍災民，共嘉惠337戶。周如意與女性志工們一起為女性災民送上物資卡，然後送上溫暖的擁抱。攝影：Mohammed Nimr Al Jamal

攝影：王素真

馳援難民的路 將一直走下去

陳樹微（慮暉）

慈濟德國志工

陳樹微

馳援難民的路，
將一直走下去

「戰爭對無辜的人
很殘忍……我們來
協助，希望這些人
不要有憎恨的心，
讓他們知道在戰爭
的殘忍外，還有人
在關心他們。」

從二〇一六年起，就和德國裔丈夫范德祿（Rudi Willi Pfaff）前往塞爾維亞（Serbia）關懷國際難民的陳樹微，對戰爭的殘酷、難民的愁苦再熟悉不過。

「我先生後來癌症過世了，他生前在加護病房告訴我，要我繼續做慈濟，連同他的那份一起。先生往生後沒多久俄烏戰爭就爆發了，證嚴上人要我『包袱啊款款耶（臺語：收拾行囊）』進入波蘭。」剛喪偶的六十四歲家庭主婦，從德國前往波蘭。

思念和哀傷，帶著服務難民的豐富經歷和丈夫生前的祝福，

九個小時的車程後，陳樹微成為第一位進入波蘭的歐洲慈濟志工：「逃出來的多是婦女帶著孩子……看到她們，我覺得自己很幸福。我先生是癌症第四期，所以他往生時我是有心理準備的，但她們沒有！帶著幼小的小孩，也許今天、明天或什麼時候，接獲先生在戰場往生的消息……因為這樣，我內心充滿感恩，可以跟這些婦女在一起。雖然真的很疲累，但我心裡沒有想說會遇到什麼困難，就覺得我能做多少、是多少。」

到達盧布林後，陳樹微立刻拿出不屈不撓的精神，天天三顧茅廬「明愛會」在波蘭的總部（註：Caritas，由上百個天主教公益團體組成的國際慈善組織），不厭其煩地介紹慈濟，從一開始彼此不熟悉，到後來迅速跨越語言、宗教隔閡，開展大規模急難救助。如今「明愛會」已把慈濟當家人，進一步推動中長期難民服務，重點對象放在長者和弱勢家庭。「我們一個月發放三到四次物資

給長者，至於行動不便的，就有留學生和明愛會志工把物資直接送上門⋯⋯我很快又要去盧布林了，聯合國難民署看我們和『明愛會』的合作，現在也希望我們能擴大發放給盧布林周遭地區的難民長者，我們得加快腳步培訓更多當地留學生加入志工行列⋯⋯」

每趟去盧布林，都是遠征，過去這段時間的密集奔波，讓年過花甲的陳樹微脊椎、腳跟都出了問題，但無論如何，馳援難民的這條路她還是會一拐一拐地走下去。

戰爭爆發後，年長者的處境往往是最艱難的，他們有語言上的障礙、健康又有問題。烏克蘭難民在自己國家看病簡單多了，只要打通電話預約，隔天就能看病。但在波蘭不同，可能要排上半年、一年才能約到專科醫師看診。而且他們還不知道要怎樣跟醫護溝通，加上不能工作，不夠健壯，沒有雇主想雇用他們⋯⋯交通也是問題，連巴士站牌都看不懂！要在波蘭久留似乎成了定局，但一切如此陌生、都要重新摸索，家人四散各地，漸漸地，長者們連寄宿家庭的房門都不敢走出一步。

長久處於害怕、憂慮、孤單，讓難民長者日益消沉二〇二二年九月底，烏克蘭裔志工漢娜提議成立「餃子俱樂部」，邀約長者每星期五到慈濟辦公室來包餃子，從此以後這個俱樂部成為慈濟在當地關懷烏克蘭難民的中長期陪伴項目之一。因為有陳樹微等人的關懷陪伴，這些家鄉味

道的餃子，已經讓他們漸漸走出了心理的陰霾，每個人的臉上也增添了燦爛的笑容。

餃子俱樂部的成立，除了給長者對外接觸的勇氣，還有信心。其中八成的餃子拿去義賣，辦公室裡的波蘭志工會購買，也會放上網站推廣。餃子有高麗菜口味，搭配炸起司、炸洋蔥、蘑菇或馬鈴薯泥，也有水果醬口味的餃子，酸櫻桃的也是特色哦！波蘭人沒吃過酸櫻桃餃子，很驚艷，所以每次都會捧場，義賣來的錢就分給這些長者，雖然不多，但他們用自己的手藝掙錢，很有成就感！

另外兩成餃子捐給慈濟的長期照顧戶，這些難民因故無法工作、經濟拮据，負擔不起享用一袋家鄉餃子的奢侈。每次給這些家庭送水餃時都會拍照，然後回來秀給俱樂部的成員看，分享這些家庭的際遇及收到餃子的開心。長者們都很欣慰，知道自己的存在還是重要的──能為他人帶去一些歡樂。

二〇二三年二月八日，陳樹微又與來自英國、義大利以及目前住在波蘭的烏克蘭籍塞爾吉奧（Sergei）等幾位慈濟志工，抵達塞爾維亞首都貝爾格勒（Belgrade），並會同十二位本土志工，前往五處距離較近的難民營送上毛毯和冬衣。這樣可以讓滯留當地的難民度過寒冷的冬季，迎接春天的到來。

長者的「餃子俱樂部」

在波蘭華沙，爐子上正煮著加了糖的大顆酸櫻桃，準備熬成漂亮的紅紫色果醬，窗外陽光正好，眼前飛灑的麵粉反射成一束束金沙，和著人群的笑聲，空氣裡酸酸的、甜甜的、暖暖的。

十幾位烏克蘭長者，一雙雙佈滿皺紋的手，靈巧地把發酵好的麵糰分成小糰子，再捍成圓形薄皮，等待櫻桃醬冷卻的同時，與大家分享自家代代相傳的Varenyky食譜（註：烏克蘭餃子）。這些長者來到這裡，就會變得像幼稚園小朋友一樣，比誰家的餃子最好。

他們把餡料和對家鄉的思念填進薄皮，捏成一個個胖墩墩的圓形或半圓形，排列整齊準備下鍋。志工懂得這些老人們言語中不容質疑的驕傲，那是流離失所四百多個日子的精神寄託，曾經以為永遠都不會變調的家庭時光……

右圖/上圖：烏克蘭長者在波蘭華沙的愛心素餃活動，2022

慈濟志工家訪後，發現這群來到波蘭的烏克蘭長者，語言與工作都有困難，生活不易，走不出家門更影響身心健康，因此志工發起了義賣烏克蘭素餃活動，邀請長者每週來包烏克蘭家鄉餃子，讓他們可以走出家門。「餃子俱樂部」因此成立。經過幾週的運作，大家配合得越來越好，有人捍皮，有人包餃子，相互合作。照片：波蘭慈濟志工提供

攝影：呂佩玲

風雪路上
肩負起信任與託付

張淑兒（慈宣）

慈濟波蘭志工

風雪路上，肩負起信任與託付

波蘭波茲南烏克蘭難民關懷，2022

為關懷因俄烏戰爭逃離烏克蘭的民眾，歐洲各國慈濟人積極連接相關資源，就近提供協助，人道救援行動正式啟動，慈濟在波蘭的盧布林、波茲南、斯塞新等地進行人道救援及物資發放。3月5日，慈濟志工張淑兒與丈夫盧卡斯(Lukasz Baranowski)，在波蘭波茲南近郊斯科熱沃政府單位提供的地點進行物資發放。照片：張淑兒提供

二〇二二年俄烏戰爭爆發後，許許多多的烏克蘭民眾為躲避戰爭而遠離家園；鄰國的波蘭，開始接收大量湧入的烏克蘭難民。二〇一八年隨波蘭籍先生定居在波茲南的臺灣人張淑兒，得知波蘭有不少難民需要幫助時，著手想要幫點忙。剛開始，張淑兒覺得自己能做的，不過就是捐點錢或捐一些二手物資就夠了。但在她拜訪了幾個烏克蘭人在波蘭波茲南（Poznań）的團體之後，發現需要幫助的狀況與案例，遠比所想像的更多、更複雜。

當得知慈濟基金會已啟動對烏克蘭難民的人道援助行動時，曾在臺灣慈濟大愛電視臺工作的張淑兒主動打電話聯繫了之前的同事，就此展開了賑災的旅程。她的這通電話串起與德國志工陳樹微的因緣，並且一步步展開與慈濟基金會的合作。

身為三個稚兒的父母，工作忙碌的張淑兒與先生盧卡斯（Lukasz Baranowski）從未接觸過難民援助，不知從何做起。於是，她經常向陳樹微請教與討論，在學習過程中，她了解了許多在其他國家救助難民的經驗，這些實務經驗的傳承，讓張淑兒意識

波蘭波茲南烏克蘭難民關懷，2022

8月13日，波蘭波茲南團隊在羅基尼察區(Rokietnica)消防局的附屬會議廳進行現值卡發放，援助當地的烏克蘭難民。穿著志工背心的烏克蘭志工為鄉親仔細核對發放資料，張淑兒(右立者)一旁陪伴，隨時支援。照片：張淑兒提供

「雖然累，但在看見烏克蘭人們接過慈濟毛毯展開笑容的那一刻，所有的辛苦都轉化為幸福。」

到許多需要解決的問題，諸如：慈濟在波蘭沒有分部，若要從他國運送物資等，必定會產生許多額外的關稅或其他費用，還有境外NGO須注意的事項等等。

記者出身的張淑兒因為過去的專業訓練，習慣主動提出問題、解決問題，因此，針對慈濟在波蘭進行援助關懷的種種困難，在她跟陳樹微幾次討論後，整理出方法。此外，波蘭東部的盧布林(Lublin)是烏克蘭人入境的第一站，因此慈濟在波蘭的關懷難民團隊，接洽了在波蘭有最大倉庫的紅十字會並開展合作。

有了可行性極高的共識後，眾人研擬出了適切的援助作法：

一、烏克蘭境內緊急救援：評估把醫療及生活物資委託波蘭盧布林紅十字會送進烏克蘭境內，救助在地受傷與需要生活物資支持的難民。

二、波蘭境內難民人道關懷：規劃把物資分送到波蘭境內接納烏克蘭難民的城市，讓在波蘭境內的烏克蘭難民免於挨餓與受凍，並提供精神上的關懷與支持。

現在，各種合約、關務、法務、政府協調、工廠寄送等等，已經難不倒波蘭的慈濟團隊了。「我們與政府機關洽談，跟不同合作單位談合約、法務，然後要協助與慈濟本會之間聯繫的翻譯，並且反覆溝通所有合約條款。」張淑兒笑著分享這段艱辛的過程，「波蘭、臺灣二地有六小時時差，所以那段時間幾乎沒有睡飽過！」

這一段經歷超乎夫妻倆的預期，但因為助人的善念，他們堅持到現在。二〇二二年三、四月，他們訪查波茲南各收容所、就地採購捐贈物資；五月起，慈濟在波茲南與紅十字會合作發放事宜，也前往鄰近城市發放。這段期間，慈濟物資與購物卡一批批運來，就存放在他們家。身為科技公司主管的盧卡斯，難以置信慈濟基金會對他們的信任，同時感受到這份委託責任重大，也更加珍惜與守護這份大愛，將每一分善款直接確實地送到受助者手中。

六月上旬，在比得哥什市進行的四場發放，是慈濟與聖文森特德保羅教堂、市政府共同合作，受助名單來自於市政府社福單位；為了確保領取人身分及追蹤得到購物卡，志工預先造冊，被通知來領取的烏克蘭難民，也必須拿著合格證件，才能完成手續領取購物卡。

早上不到九點，教堂前已經排起了長隊，難民們有的面色惆悵，有的神情不安。一位憂心忡忡的老人家，向志工詢問自己是否在發放名單內，並且跟志工反映太早來排隊肚子餓。身在現場，張淑兒目睹並深切地感受到了戰爭帶來的傷害。

六十三歲的娜塔莉亞（Nataltia Shelukhina）帶著八歲孫兒維托理（Vitalii Chernykh）前來領取發放。小男孩顯得十分不安，「孫子的父母在戰事中已經身亡，他先天就患有隱性疾病，因躲避戰亂精神狀態更加不穩定！」娜塔莉亞奶奶無奈地告知志工他們的遭遇。小男孩無法控制緊張的情緒，抓住志工的手並扣得好緊好緊，一鬆開就會不安地吼叫。張淑兒和烏克蘭志工拿

波蘭志工培訓共修課程，2023

8月1日至4日，波蘭慈濟志工齊聚波茲南會所進行培訓共修課程，由德、奧慈濟志工組成的「波蘭志工關懷團隊」，陪伴來自華沙、盧布林、波茲南、斯塞新等地的志工，進行一連四天的共修活動。波蘭志工換上代表榮譽(見習志工穿著)的灰衣，彼此鼓勵。攝影：陳樹微

「每一次有不同意見，我們總是一起討論；我會告訴烏克蘭志工們，我跟盧卡斯和你們一樣同為慈濟志工，所以大家沒有身分的區別，只是真誠地為需要的人付出而已。」

慈濟志工

著水果、麵包，一邊安撫著小男孩，一邊安慰著奶奶。老人承受著失去女兒、女婿的痛，還要帶著患病的孫子，面對無止盡的醫藥費、生活費，往後能否在異國波蘭安身，前途茫茫。看著祖孫離去的背影，張淑兒與其他志工已經淚流滿面。於是，她將祖孫提報到市政府並且記錄下來，列為中長期追蹤關懷的對象。

對待以工代賑的烏克蘭籍志工，慈濟在波蘭的難民關懷團隊也是給予同樣的信任及尊重。張淑兒表示：「每一次有不同意見，我們總是一起討論；我會告訴烏克蘭的志工，我跟盧卡斯也和你們一樣同為慈濟志工，所以大家沒有身分的分別，真誠地為需要的人付出而已。」

在發放期間不斷遇到善良的人主動幫助，提供發放場所、協助搬運物資、送來食物茶點、居中聯繫溝通、一起設法尋找資源等等。張淑兒說：「在過程中，一直遇到很棒的人，所以我們越做越開心。」正因為每個人都願意承擔一小部分，才讓整個事情可以圓滿！」因為發放關懷行動，他們現在已成為好朋友，更是相互依靠的好夥伴，也讓烏克蘭志工們有更多情感上的連結，了解自己雖處異鄉並不孤單。

面對戰爭給人所帶來的外在和內心的摧殘，身在波蘭的張淑兒更願意肩負起慈濟的一份信任與託付，為這些難民帶來繼續生活下去的信心和勇氣！

波蘭波茲南烏克蘭難民關懷，2023

去年慈濟捐贈給波蘭波茲南紅十字會的睡袋仍有庫存，因此1月17日，慈濟波茲南團隊與波茲南紅十字會一起合作發放物資給2022年10月後抵達波蘭、急需幫忙的烏克蘭家庭。照片：張淑兒提供

攝影：游錫璋

持續愛的付出

帶動善的循環

陳秋華（濟暉）

慈濟約旦志工

慈濟約旦分會執行長

慈濟志工

73

陳秋華

持續愛的付出，帶動善的循環

這是一個多災多難的世界。自二十世紀起，戰火一直在中東地區燃燒，埃及、敘利亞、伊拉克等阿拉伯國家連續不斷進行了多次大規模戰爭，各國之間的戰火此消彼長，從未停止。伴隨戰爭的是無數無辜的百姓流離失所、無家可歸、餓殍遍野……

這一天，在約旦和伊拉克邊境的魯威西（Ruwaished）難民營，哀嚎遍野中，一名身材魁偉的東方男子聽見一陣陣孩子哇哇叫的哭聲，那是一種撕心裂肺的飢餓與恐慌的呼喊。他毫不猶豫，迅速朝哭聲跑去。出現在他眼前的是飢餓的難民們瞪大著恐慌和無助的眼睛，一群餓極了的孩子發出嘶啞無力的哭叫聲……

他捷步走向一個脫水的蘇丹孩子，由於長期飢餓，細細瘦瘦的四肢無力地耷拉著，已奄奄一息。他抱起這個垂死的孩子，飛奔向附近的野戰醫院。一趟又一趟，他不記得自己跑了多少趟，救出了多少瀕臨死亡的兒童。

二〇〇三年，伊拉克戰爭突然爆發，戰火延燒至二〇一一年。

約旦與伊拉克邊境，一群被戰火包夾而無藏身之地的無辜百姓發出絕望的呼救。在挨挨擠擠的難民中，人們又見到了這位東方男子，他帶著一支救援的隊伍出現在那裡，在廢墟荒野，為難民們搭建起一個個帳篷。見到難民們拖著疲憊的身軀住進了臨時的家，他又轉身與他的志工團隊，向這批極度飢餓的人們送上麵包糧食和水⋯⋯

顯然，這位身材偉岸的東方男子不是第一次出現在難民營，在災難深重的中東災區，在被戰火摧毀的城市廢墟、荒漠和山村，只要有難民流離失所，人們總能見到他。忙碌穿梭的身影，謙卑的微笑，他說著一口流利的當地語言，雙手合十，向災民們送上安慰與祝福。無論他們是居無定所的游牧民族，還是流落在中東的非裔人，或因戰爭逃離家園的難民，無論他們屬於哪個宗教，在這位東方男子的眼裡，每一個人都是活生生的生命，每一個人都有不死的願望，他唯有向他們伸出救助的雙手，拯救每一個他所遇見的生命。

人們親切地稱呼這位東方男子⋯MR. CHEN。

陳秋華，中東地區約旦慈濟負責人。

陳秋華並非生來就是大慈大悲的慈濟人；他祖籍彰化，在苗栗長大，從小便是個頗出風頭的小孩。一九六七年，當時在士校就讀的陳秋華，由於嚴格的自我要求，榮任為跆拳班教官，一九七三年代表中華隊參加了首屆世界盃跆拳錦標賽同時榮膺隊長，隨後晉級為響噹噹的黑帶高手。

一九七四年，陳秋華奉派到約旦培訓當時的國王侍衛隊、教導宗室成員練跆拳，以及協助約旦發展跆拳道運動。一九九九年，當時的約旦國王過世後，陳秋華便一直保護著國王御弟哈山親王一家安危，既是哈山親王的隨身帶槍侍衛，也與哈山親王亦師亦友，在當地可謂呼風喚雨的人物。

那時，陳秋華笑稱自己：難免「少年輕狂」。

一直以來，陳秋華都感激太太把他領進慈濟的大門。他回憶，那還是一九九七年，太太帶他認識慈濟，當他初見慈濟是由一群婦人組織時，還不以為然。雖然慈濟有不殺生、不偷盜、不飲酒等十戒，他還是大口喝酒、大塊吃肉，有時能夠「一天喝掉八瓶酒，吃肉撐到坐也不是、躺也不是」。但某一天之後，事情就有了改變，酒肉穿腸過的陳秋華，突然脫胎換骨換了一個人。

那是他返臺參加慈濟全球志工幹部研習，初見到證嚴上人。印象深刻的是，他剛上完研習中的一堂骨髓捐贈課程，動員人們

捐贈骨髓本來就猶如沙漠上插柳那麼艱難，陳秋華滿心好奇慈濟或說由證嚴上人帶領的慈濟是怎麼做到的？隨後，當證嚴上人出現在講臺上，他如同被電擊了一般，渾身震撼：這麼一位瘦弱的女子，卻在一九六六年創辦了佛教克難慈濟功德會，帶領三十位家庭婦女，每天省下五角錢，投入竹筒，並與五位弟子每人每天多做一些手工、加工品來賣，這些點滴累積的存款或收入就是慈濟救助苦難人的來源，硬是在物欲橫流的社會環境中，克己、克勤、克儉、克難地打開一條關愛天下受難者的慈濟之路。

那天在講臺上，證嚴上人輕柔且堅定的聲音卻如同驚雷在會場響起。要成立一個骨髓庫，她講道，這很困難──除了需要龐大的資金，也要很多專家學者的協助，更重要的是必須有人願意捐贈骨髓；從呼籲、驗血、配對到進行骨髓移植手術，過程中變數很大，捐髓者如果在最後一秒反悔，將會前功盡棄……

陳秋華驚得目瞪口呆，這太難了，但是證嚴上人溫柔的目光中卻閃爍著信念與決心，儘管事情艱難，但師父堅信，本著尊重生命的信念，必會有愛心人士響應。

「尊重生命」，證嚴上人所講的四個字，如同棒槌敲打著他沉積了四十七年的世俗溫床，淚眼漣漪中他問自己：「我活到四十七歲，為這個社會做了什麼？證嚴上人雖然那麼瘦弱，悲願卻那麼大。而我的人生意義在哪裡？」

約旦安曼照顧戶發放暨往診活動，2017

慈濟志工前往安曼帳篷區探訪游牧民族貝都因照顧戶，
並進行往診。小男孩將竹筒撲滿交給志工時，裡面的銅
板聲打動約旦分會負責人陳秋華的心。攝影：游錫璋

「尊重生命」，證嚴上人所講的四個字，如同棒槌敲打著他沉積了四十七年的世俗溫床，淚眼漣漪中他問自己：「上人那麼瘦弱，悲願卻那麼大。而我的人生意義在哪裡？」

自此以後他告別了酒肉，在中東豎起了慈濟的大旗，在信仰中找到了心靈的皈依，在他生活的地方，度化當地人並落實慈悲宏願。

二○○三年，美伊戰爭後，陳秋華前往約旦與伊拉克邊境為難民設立帳篷、發放食物，並到醫院關懷被戰火波及而受傷的無辜民眾。戰後，中東地區難民患有許多罕見疾病，陳秋華帶著懸壺濟世的人文關懷，為他們送醫、送藥，甚至在必要時將他們送上手術臺治療，而術後為了患者的康復，他除了代表慈濟進行捐贈，更是身先士卒帶頭自掏腰包，僅在二○一六年三月到二○一九年八月，直接受他救濟的患者已超過一千三百例，其中百分之九十七為敘利亞難民兒童。

直到今天，中東地區的砲火飛彈依然不斷狂轟濫炸，傷害著無以計數的無辜人民。陳秋華帶著他的志工團隊又出發了，為飽受戰火蹂躪的難民們搭建帳篷，捐贈和籌集食物和生活必需物品，給難民們緊急食物發放，為他們送醫、送藥，並幫助失學的孩子重新得到教育的機會……這些都成了他的生命的一部分。

對於陳秋華，這位常年穿梭在中東難民營區的慈濟負責人來說，愛與慈悲，不是肌膚之親，一蔬一飯是一種不可摧毀的意志，是濟愛天下的英雄夢想。他堅信：「持續不斷地付出愛，一定會帶動善的循環。」

上圖：約旦敘利亞難民關懷，2016

慈濟志工前往安曼東部Hadalat區，鄰近敘利亞邊境，關懷難民及聯合國兒童基金會(UNICEF)收留的敘利亞孩童，並發放生活物資。圖：志工合力將物資搬下車。攝影：陳秋華

右圖上：約旦馬夫拉克札塔里發放活動，2018

慈濟志工發放生活物資給敘利亞難民及當地照顧戶游牧民族貝都因(Bedouin)人。雨後地上泥濘，志工鞋子沾黏滿了泥巴。
攝影：游錫璋

右圖下：約旦敘利亞難民關懷義診及發放活動，2016

慈濟志工前往馬夫拉克札塔里難民營營外帳篷散戶區關懷，發放文具用品及冬衣外套予難民孩童。物資貧乏，寒冬中小朋友僅穿拖鞋或破舊的鞋子。照片：慈濟約旦分會提供

照片：林綠卿提供

化身陽光
溫暖失根異鄉人

林綠卿（懿弘）
慈濟約旦志工

林綠卿

化身陽光，溫暖失根異鄉人

「拜託，發放時，請你們一定要彎下身體，雙手交付物資。與他們有眼神的交流，請給他們最溫暖的笑容與尊重。」

早年移民約旦的林綠卿（Lamiya Lin），在二〇二〇年九月加入慈濟約旦分會後，開始接觸並全身心投入對敘利亞難民的救助和關懷。多年來，林綠卿長期陪伴難民個案，幫助敘利亞單親媽媽自力更生，身為兩個孩子母親的她，特別關注難民兒童的醫療與教育。

林綠卿總是用笑容面對每一個人，熱情、真摯、極富同理心的她，像一縷陽光，給難民們失根在異鄉的生活，注入了更多溫暖與希望。

以下為慈濟大愛人文中心（TCC）對林綠卿（林）的採訪整理，發表前經由受訪者審校。

TCC：第一次接觸難民時，您的感受是什麼？

林：第一次到馬弗拉克省（Mafraq）虎威賈村（Huweyia）發放防疫物資時，看到難民孩子們都沒穿鞋，讓我很震驚。可是孩子臉上都是真誠開心的笑容，物資缺乏對他們來說彷彿並沒有影響。可是大人們就不一樣了，他們臉上、手上布滿風霜，看起來疲憊憔悴，收到物資後，眼神裡充滿著對慈濟志工的感激與善意。

當和他們眼神對視，我似乎感受到這些年來的辛苦，逃離家園的無奈和寄人籬下的委屈。我對年輕志工們說：「拜託，發放時，請你們一定要彎下身體，雙手交付物資。與他們有眼神的交流，請給他們最溫暖的笑容與尊重。」許多人視難民為包袱，這些人受苦很久了，很長一段時間被當作次等人看待。異鄉人的心理折磨與孤單，以及被輕視的傷害，不是我們這些安住家園的有福之人可以想像的，他們的不安全感雖然沒有說出口，卻刺痛了我的心。

TCC：在這麼多年的難民關懷和救助裡，您記憶中最閃耀的片段以及最艱難的時光？

林：今年我們帶著「慈心之家」（註：慈濟從二〇一三年關懷的三十六戶敘利亞難民單親媽媽和孩子，長期贊助房租及學生助學金。）的孩子們打包文具書包時，雖然他們只有十、十一、十二歲，卻懂得感恩慈濟與證嚴上人，懂得感恩有做善事的機會。身為長期陪伴的慈濟志工之一，我感到很欣慰，因

上圖：約旦馬夫拉克嚴冬送暖柴火發放，2021

約旦冬天晚上非常的寒冷，住在沙漠中帳篷區的人們更是面臨低溫酷寒；慈濟志工經訪視了解，根據不同帳篷區居民生活習慣，採買木柴及橄欖籽渣壓製的煤球，在寒流來臨前進行發放。圖：虎威賈村(Huweyia)的小孩們一起聚在火爐前烤火。
攝影：林綠卿

右圖：約旦安曼貝橋學校文具發放，2023

開學日將近，約旦慈濟志工前往安曼貝橋學校為貧困家庭的學生發放學用品。左起：慈濟敘利亞籍志工如思（Mohammad Khair Roz）、林綠卿、約旦籍志工哈達(Khader Khalifah)以恭敬的心，雙手將學用品遞給學生。攝影：劉金玫

最艱難也是最覺悟的時刻是陪伴醫療個案，看到生離死別，見證無常。看到十四歲罹患骨癌的難民兒童離世，聽到她的母親的哭喊聲，跟荒漠的寒風呼嘯交雜，那種撕心裂肺的悲鳴，讓我了解到生命就在一呼一吸之間，爭是非，爭對錯，對比人命的脆弱，實在沒有什麼值得花心思的。

還曾經見證過恩愛夫妻無法白頭，可是他們是幸福的，因為一直到死亡將他們分開，他們都深深愛戀著彼此。藉境借鏡，世間人教世間法，這些大哉教育的菩薩們，他們用生命最後一段時光與我結緣，走進了我的生命，令我深深感恩他們。

TCC：敘利亞在約旦的難民中，有很多婦女和小孩，同為女性，對於她們現在的處境，您有什麼感想？

林：敘利亞的單親媽媽們在先生缺席的情況下，必須要承擔起父親的角色，養家的同時還要教育孩子。除了擔心生計，擔心孩子教育問題，她們可以說是犧牲了這一輩子的幸福，保護陪伴她們的孩子長大。以前無憂無慮單純的家庭主婦生活已不復返，身為難民，可以依靠的就是她們的雙手。慈濟約旦分會在二〇二三年五月開始，提供四個不同的職訓課程，可以工作養家學會自力更生，成為孩子們的好榜樣。

為善的種子已經在孩子心中種下，並且開始發芽。而「慈心之家」的媽媽們，跟著我們一起到偏鄉送愛心時，她們用媽媽的心去膚慰當地貧戶的孩子，愛灑的菩薩身影令人感動。

TCC：近一段時間，慈濟約旦分會在救助和關懷敘利亞難民方面有什麼新的進展？

林：在南薩與安曼地區，有些感恩戶我們已經照顧長達十一年，她們的孩子也適應了約旦環境，很多還完成了大學教育，開始工作。所以志工團隊在二〇二三年五月開始進行家訪，深入了解每一戶家庭現在的狀況。如果家庭已經有自力更生的能力，我們就會停止每月的救濟金發放，轉而去幫助其他急需的家庭。而一些孤寡、殘疾和年老無收入的家庭，慈濟會繼續關懷。現在許多國際組織退出了，難民的處境依舊辛苦，尤其對沒有謀生能力的家庭來說很殘酷。

TCC：您對未來難民關懷和救助的期望？

林：醫療與教育將是持續關懷和救助的重點。唯有教育，可以幫助下一代翻轉人生。而貧病相依的人生是真實苦，所以慈濟人醫會義診不會間斷，幫助對象以十八歲以下的孩子為重點。

孩子是未來的希望，要讓他們受教育，要培養慈悲心，要教導他們知足感恩，還要有開闊胸襟去包容不同文化，有同理心以及正信正念。同時也希望這些在約旦長大的敘利亞孩子們可以更好的融入約旦社會，在未來可以自發地去幫助別人。

約旦分會「土敘地震救援」，2023

土耳其、敘利亞於2月6日發生芮氏規模7.8強震，造成嚴重災情。約旦臺商的駱駝成衣廠，
捐贈成衣和毛毯給慈濟約旦分會，慈濟與哈希米組織(JHCO)合作，委由約旦軍方將物資載
往敘利亞邊界，再由聯合國租用的車子在邊界接貨，運進敘利亞送往災區，發放給地震受
災戶。2月28日，哈希米組織的倉庫出動四輛約旦軍方卡車，裝載物資準備運往敘國邊界。
圖：林綠卿在軍方卡車上綁上慈濟logo布條。 照片：慈濟約旦分會提供

用愛
穿越一條禁行路

敘利亞籍慈濟志工
約旦「慈心之家」負責人

如思

8月12日，慈濟約旦分會志工從安曼出發到馬夫拉克二地進行食物發放。志工長期關懷馬夫拉克第一區札塔里(Za'atari)本土貝都因(Bedouin)帳篷區，為貝都因人發放物資；來自慈心之家(Tzu Xin House)的志工梨娜(Lena，著志工背心中)引導孩子們依序排隊，並為其送上蛋糕、飲料、蘋果。這些雖是平常不過的食物，但在貧困地區孩子眼中是無比的美味。攝影：Asmaa Akhras

「自從戰爭發生後，所有敘利亞人才知道，有安全感是多麼可貴。當我們有信心可以回到祖國安全生活時，我們就會回去，哪怕住在帳篷裡也好。我們多希望停止戰爭，重回和平。」

如思
用愛，
穿越一條禁行路

「看！那就是敘利亞(Syria)！」敘利亞籍志工如思(Mohammad Khair Roz)指著約旦賈比爾(Jabir)邊界關哨另一邊的土地，興奮地向一同前往的慈濟約旦分會志工林綠卿和哈達(Khader Khalifeh)說道：「快！快幫我拍照！」說話時雙眼噙滿了淚水，手指的方向正是他日思夜想卻無法返回的家與國。

二○二三年二月二十八日，對如思來說是難忘的一天，對慈濟而言更是具有里程碑意義的一天。在土敘大地震三個禮拜後，突破重重困難，透過約旦軍方，臺灣國華紡織約旦分公司「駱駝成衣工廠」捐贈了兩輛軍用卡車的衣服和毛毯，終於成功送進敘利亞。這是慈濟物資首度成功進入敘利亞，從邊界到倉庫，雖然只有短短十分鐘的車程，卻是慈濟賑災史上突破性的一步。

如思的父親出生在敘利亞大馬士革的貧民區，以替人修鞋維生，但他憑著努力學習，最終獲得了阿拉伯文學、伊斯蘭法和法律三個學士學位，甚至成為大馬士革大學著名的學者。在他的父親往生時，大馬士革一半的人口紛紛走上街頭參加他的告別式。如思說：「父親的故事，鼓勵我努力學習和工作。」

一九八二年，敘利亞發生哈馬政治危機。一九九〇年，如思離開家鄉去杜拜，在杜拜當了十七年的阿拉伯語老師。二〇〇七年，他回到敘利亞，開了一家出版公司。四年後，二〇一一年敘利亞戰爭爆發，試圖再到杜拜找份工作未果後，如思只得帶著家人來到了約旦。起初全家人同住在札塔里（Za'atari）難民營，之後搬到了安曼。

離開家鄉十二年裡，如思再也沒能踏進身後的故土。他內心那個曾經美麗富饒、這個世界上最古老、人類文明發源地之一的祖國，經過十二年內戰後支離破碎、物資匱乏。以往物資豐饒的祖國捐贈物資來救濟他國，現在卡車方向轉向，吃穿都依靠別人資助……

慈濟志工

89

二○一二年，四位富有的敘利亞商人租下約旦首都安曼（Amman）市郊的一棟二十二戶公寓，用於收容敘利亞內戰中失去丈夫的寡婦和她們的孩子，並起名為「採法德之家」（Bait Al Safoud）。原本大家以為戰爭很快就能結束，可到了二○一六年，依舊沒有停止的跡象。而商人們也變成了難民，越來越難以繼續支撐租金的負擔，於是想辦法尋求幫助。透過一位慈濟志工的介紹，二○一六年十二月，慈濟約旦志工們便帶著食物包第一次到了那裡，彼時，如思便是公寓的負責人。

「第一次和慈濟接觸時，就覺得這個慈善組織很不一樣。你能感覺他們真的關心你，把別人的小孩當成自己的小孩。」會面後，如思詢問是否下個月可以再來，就這樣，「採法德之家」在慈濟資助租金後逐漸穩定，慈濟持續提供義診、物資發放並贊助學費等，這棟樓也在二○一七年改名為「慈心之家」。在志工陳秋華（註：慈濟約旦分會執行長）的帶動下，如思也成為一名慈濟志工。

經由居住在約旦的慈濟志工援助，「慈心之家」已經入住了三十三戶人家，除了為他們提供教育和醫療上的幫助外，慈濟還為一些單親媽媽們開辦了四個職業培訓班：裁縫、美容美髮、居家看護和烹飪。授人以魚不如授人以漁，這些技能可以讓她們在約旦過上自給自足的生活。

二○二三年二月六日，一場慘烈的地震，在土耳其東南接壤敘利亞西北邊境地帶發生。強烈的地震摧毀了成千上萬棟建築，數萬人喪生，即使幸運逃生，無數人也不得不暴露在冬季寒冷的惡劣天候中。沒水、沒電、沒有足夠的禦寒衣物和食物，日子異常難捱。

因為敘利亞政府與反對派之間的武裝衝突已逾十年，敘利亞西北部共有四百一十萬人依靠人道援助維生。地震發生後，敘利亞中央政府強烈要求所有救援行動和物資由他們決定；錯綜複雜的政治環境導致西北地區面臨極大的人道危機，而敘利亞人民則成為政治角力下無辜的受害者。

「地震發生後的第二天，當我來到辦公室時，驚訝地發現陳秋華師兄已經開始計劃找物資送進敘利亞。當他說可以開始打包慈濟採購的物資時，不僅我很興奮，『慈心之家』的媽媽和小孩們也很激動。我們終於可以為在敘利亞的同胞們做點什麼了。」如思回憶起當時的情景，臉上還是抑制不住喜悅。從二月十九日起，有十八位「慈心之家」的媽媽和孩子，每天五個小時用來為災區的敘利亞鄉親打包物資。當志工問小朋友們累不累時，他們說：「我們願意為災民付出而辛苦，因為我們是一家人。」儘管對許多年幼的孩童來說，敘利亞只是個印象模糊的祖國，但在慈濟美善的滋養下，在他們幼小的心靈裡，已種下了無私大愛的種子。

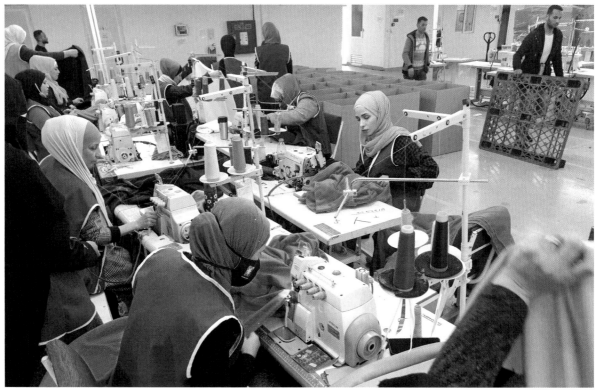

約旦分會「土敘地震救援」，2023

上圖：「慈心之家」的媽媽為遠在三百多英哩外災區的敘利亞鄉親打包，打包工作並不輕鬆，但大家為能幫到同胞而開心。攝影：穆罕默德·法尤米

下圖：土敘邊境大震後，約旦駱駝成衣廠的工人們趕工裁縫，兩個星期內為敘利亞境內的災民完成五萬條毛毯。攝影：張明傑

二月二十八日這一天，四輛掛著慈濟標誌布條的軍用卡車載著第一批物資駛向十五公里外的賈比爾邊界關哨。慈濟志工林綠卿、哈達和如思站在邊界關哨口，目送車隊緩緩駛入敘利亞。雖然進入敘利亞境內後布條必須拿下、由於政策的限制和安全考量，慈濟志工無法親送，但依舊無法消滅他們內心的沸騰——慈濟終於進入敘利亞了！

如思看著著卡車進入邊界，慢慢往敘利亞深處開，當下百感交集：「我的三個姊妹還在敘利亞，我們已經十二年沒見了，很想念她們。我曾經在敘利亞的一切都沒了，沒有理由回去，而且回去了就回不來了。」如思道出了數以百萬逃離在外的敘利亞人心聲，每一句話都那麼沈重。流落他鄉，如思已經將心安在了當下，因為這裡還有更多的事情要做。

國土有界，大愛無疆。未來，那條到賈比爾邊界關哨的禁行路，慈濟能帶著愛和關懷親自走過去。

「以前我也有和其他慈善組織接觸，總覺得缺了點什麼。直到和慈濟一起做發放時，志工們一直向受助者道感謝，感謝他們接受了我們的物資，我終於找到那個點，原來付出該是這個樣子。我學到了慈善真正的精神，學到了怎麼真正能與人結善緣。」

約旦馬夫拉克札塔里發放活動，2017

慈濟志工關懷因戰亂逃難到約旦的敘利亞難民，前往馬夫拉克札塔里難民營營外帳篷散戶區，發放生活物資予難民家庭，及札塔里照顧戶游牧民族貝都因人。攝影：游錫璋

右圖：約旦分會「土敘地震救援」，2023

2月26日是歷史性的一日。五貨櫃滿載慈濟捐贈的成衣、毛毯以及其他救援物資的卡車終於能夠進入敘利亞。這批物資委由約旦軍方載往敘利亞邊界，再由聯合國租用的車子在邊界接貨，運進敘利亞送往災區，發放給地震受災戶。照片：慈濟約旦分會提供

阿富汗賑災，2002

慈濟與美國騎士橋國際救援組織(KBI)援助阿富汗，馳援飽受旱災、內戰及阿富汗戰爭之苦的民眾。艾巴克市廢墟難民發放，難民有秩序地等待領取物資。攝影：黃思賢

看到溫馨

愛，是人間之寶；

心中有愛，

就會時時看到人間溫馨動人的情景。

——證嚴上人靜思語

根繫何處：

慈濟國際難民援助特展

UPROOTED: the Exhibition

慈濟國際難民援助特展，2023

展覽名稱「UPROOTED」（根繫何處），在陽光的映射下投影在慈濟大愛人文中心展廳的地面上，地面也成為了圖像展示的一部分。攝影：葉子

慈悲足跡的印證——

慈濟國際難民援助特展

曾慈慧（慈璟）

慈濟美國總會執行長

慈濟人秉持著證嚴上人「無緣大慈、同體大悲」的教誨，在二〇二三年的「全球難民論壇」的年會前，就《全球難民契約》核心安排、推出一系列的新移民、難民、政治庇護的經驗探討，慈濟在其中也分享了援助與陪伴受助者的作法，展現慈善無疆界的信念，亦是慈悲足跡的印證。證嚴上人憂懷天下，即使深感深知慈濟的付出可能只是杯水車薪、微不足道，雖然也不免壓力沉重，但也絕對不放棄，願為苦難蒼生盡最大的心力。

佛法在人間，就是要在人間行菩薩道，天下的米籮會由慈濟人一起來挑。

「全球難民論壇」每四年舉辦一次，它聚集了各國難民收容社區的專家、私營部門、民間信仰組織、政府機構和學術界的研究人員，以及其他在支持難民方面可以發揮作用的專家及組織代表，為支持對難民的全面應對措施，並最終實現契約的目標利益，提供了一個分享良好經驗並承諾提供財政支持、技術專長和政策變動的平臺。

首屆全球難民論壇於二〇一九年十二月十六日至十八日在日內瓦舉行，有三千多人參加，並達成約一千百四百項的承諾，提供財政、物資、技術和政策支持，以及重新安置地點的規劃或其他解決途徑的可能。

慈濟在二〇二三年的全球難民論壇開展前在慈濟大愛人文中心（Tzu Chi Center）推出「根繫何處：流離失所後的慈悲共渡——慈濟國際難民援助特展」（UPROOTED: Compassion After Displacement—Tzu Chi Global Refugee Relief Exhibition），旨在邀請國際社會關注，倡導共同承擔長期公平收容難民的責任，以及安排未來規劃。這是團隊的工作與努力，需要所有相關者的合作和參與。（我們）想要傳遞一個信息：「隨時做好準備，當情況出現時，當挑戰來臨時，嘗試用慈悲及同理心，去面對它，找到解決方案，一起去解決。」

展覽呈現了慈濟在波蘭援助烏克蘭難民，以及在約旦和塞爾維亞援助敘利亞難民的點點滴滴；土耳其滿納海國際學校（El Menahil International School）學生們的七十三幅畫作被精心安排，從下至上，畫作由暗轉亮，觀眾能感受到孩子們心境的改變與轉折；展覽還包括了對泰國難民的醫療照顧、馬來西亞難民的身心靈關懷專案。進入第三層展廳，佛陀的足跡和慈濟的緣起在觀眾眼前緩緩展開，整個特展娓娓道來慈濟四十多年來，在全球推動難民人道援助工作的故事。

聯合國兒童基金會美國分會的專案主任（Chief Program Officer, UNICEF USA）達拉·席爾瓦（Darla Silva）說：「我今天學到了關於慈悲的一課，這（解決國際難民人道危機）是一場充滿力量的全球性運動，我們很榮幸能攜手為此努力。」

每一幀照片、創作、文字、影片，背後所承載的故事，就是巨大的慈悲能量的最佳見證。歡迎大家共同留下足跡。

慈濟國際難民援助特展，2023

右圖：6月13日，開幕儀式上，美國總會執行長曾慈慧為來賓說明展覽的意涵。攝影：Héctor Muniente

左圖：俄烏戰爭導致幾百萬烏克蘭居民流離失所，證嚴上人在得知這個消息後，發動全球慈濟人共同心繫烏克蘭民眾，並伸出援手。展覽中展示證嚴上人為烏克蘭難民寫的信和慈濟為難民發放的現值卡。攝影：Philip Hwang

翻頁：6月13日，70餘位特邀嘉賓及慈濟志工出席開幕典禮。受邀出席的有聯合國兒童基金會美國分會、世界宗教議會、紐約市警察局社區事務局、紐約州長辦公室、國際佛光協會、紐約土耳其文化中心、巴哈國際社團等機構的代表。賓客一一參觀了大樓的三層樓，進一步了解慈濟全球難民救援工作以及慈濟的歷史和理念。攝影(排序從上至下，從右至左)：Héctor Muniente/劉輝/ Héctor Muniente/羅奇華/ Héctor Muniente/劉輝/郭恩璞/郭恩璞/劉輝

Дорогі українці,

З невимовним жалем у серці я пишу цього листа від імені «Цу Чи», міжнародної гуманітарної благодійної організації зі штаб-квартирою у Тайвані. З новин ми дізналися, що дуже багато людей вимушено покинули Україну через війну. Без сумнівів, ваша подорож була справжнім випробуванням, але завдяки неабиякій силі та наполегливості, ви тепер у безпеці. Ми з вами у цей нелегкий час. Знайте, що весь світ об'єднався і працює аби надати вам необхідну підтримку.

Наша організація була створена на основі буддійської віри у велику любов. Наші волонтери в Польщі та у інших Європейських країнах організовують постачання та співпрацюють з людьми та організаціями доброї волі, щоб надати вам комплексну підтримку. Хоча нинішні умови не дозволяють нам реалізувати доставку товарів у більших масштабах, але ми хочемо, щоб ви знали, що наші зусилля втілюють любов багатьох людей, які піклуються про вас. Наші волонтери за межами Європи також долучаються до надання допомоги та моляться за вас. Ми молимося за ваш душевний спокій та мир у світі.

Я приєднуюсь до волонтерів «Цу Чи» з усіх куточків світу та сердечно дарую вам нашу любов і благословення. Я щиро бажаю аби ми усі залишалися мужніми та не втрачали надію. Нашими молитвами та вірою ми наблизимо час, коли всі українці зможуть повернутися додому і до мирного життя.

Бажаю вам здоров'я, миру та маю надію на світ, де більше не буде біди.

Шіх Ченг Йен
Засновник
Буддійський благодійний фонд Цу Чи (Tzu Chi)
Березень, 2022

Dear Ukrainian Friends,

It is with a very heavy heart that I write this letter on behalf of Tzu Chi, a global humanitarian charity organization based in Taiwan. In news reports, we have seen countless people being forced to leave their homeland due to the war in Ukraine. The journey must have been a challenging one, but with tremendous courage and perseverance, you have now arrived at a safe place. Our hearts go out to you, and we stand by you. We want you to know that people around the world are working together to support you.

Our organization was founded on the Buddhist spirit of great love. Our volunteers in Poland and throughout Europe are assembling supplies and partnering with kindhearted people and organizations to provide you with support. Although we cannot send many supplies in the current environment, we want you to know that our efforts embody the love of many people who care about you. Outside of Europe, our volunteers are also supporting the relief efforts from afar and offering their sincere prayers. We pray that you will have peace of mind and that there will be peace in the world.

With deepest sincerity in my heart, I join Tzu Chi volunteers around the world to offer our love and blessings. May we all find courage and hope. I pray and have faith that, in time, you can return to your homes and to a peaceful life.

I wish you health, peace, and a world free of disasters.

Shih Cheng Yen
Founder
Buddhist Tzu Chi Charity Foundation
March, 2022

Цу Чи (Tzu Chi) турбується про вас
Tzu Chi Cares for You

不安困惑中的穩定力量：「慈濟國際難民援助特展」的策展理念

范婷（明斐）慈濟美國總會文史室主任

慈濟國際難民援助特展，2023

展覽前言牆。攝影：范婷

二○一九年二月，證嚴上人鼓勵美國慈濟人為土耳其「滿納海國際學校」募心募愛，於是我和我們的影視團隊來到土耳其伊斯坦堡拍攝紀錄。在滿納海國際學校裡，和敘利亞難民孩子與學校老師朝夕相處的日日夜夜，滿滿的感動在心裡。二○一九年十月十三日，位於紐約曼哈頓的「慈濟大愛人文中心」正式開幕啟用，我心裡默默的想著，如果「滿納海國際學校」的故事，可以在這裡展出，會是多麼美好的事！

世事難料，時間倏忽來到二○二二年二月，俄烏戰爭爆發，四月我們前往波蘭開始烏克蘭難民的援助行動。烏克蘭人的美麗、優雅，一群可愛的人，卻不得不離鄉背井，但心繫故土。他們的掙扎無助，令人心疼。慈濟在那裡，提供即時經濟上的援助，還有心靈的陪伴。這一趟波蘭行，我心中又不禁想著，是否慈濟陪伴烏克蘭難民的點滴，能在慈濟大愛人文中心展出？

於是，當慈濟大愛人文中心決定要進行「慈濟國際難民援助特展」時，我和團隊興奮地提供第一手的紀錄片、照片和文字。終於，慈濟在世界各地進行的難民援助行動，能在紐約曼哈頓這個世界窗口被看見！

我們為這個特展命名：「根繫何處：流離失所後的慈悲共渡」（UPROOTED: Compassion After Displacement），希望藉此展現一股正能量和希望。「Uprooted」，人們被迫離開自己的家鄉，充滿無奈與不安，但「Compassion After Displacement」，是我們真正想要強調的，是慈濟四十多年來在世界各地進行難民人道救援行動，將悲憫之心付諸行動，陪伴這群離開了家鄉到異鄉的人們，紮根並展開新生活。

我們的特展視覺策展人蘇曉玲（Ling Soo），加入「Mirror Vinyl」這種鏡面反光貼紙（乙烯基薄膜）的元素，在展場的不同區域出現。做為一個反思視角，當人們參觀展覽時，會從反光貼紙中看到自己的臉，但極為模糊。而模糊的視野，正是反映出難民對於未來的困惑和不確定感。同時，選擇以壓克力板（Acrylic sheet）取代相框，沒有一般相框的框架，自然地跟白色牆壁相連在一起，照片具有延展性，不被相框給局限住，表達出難民的未來是有無限希望的。

整個展覽的基調雖然有著戰爭無情的背景，但我們挑選照片時，每張照片都是一個故事，是一場又一場溫情的湧動，是一份互助的情誼，以及慈濟人帶給流離失所的難民和帶給慈濟人自己的——一份向上的力量。

展覽中展出七十三張從土耳其滿納海國際學校快遞寄送到紐約的繪畫作品。不加任何修飾，這些學生們的畫作直接呈現在一樓展廳入口處以及二樓的牆上。每一張繪畫的背後，都有著一

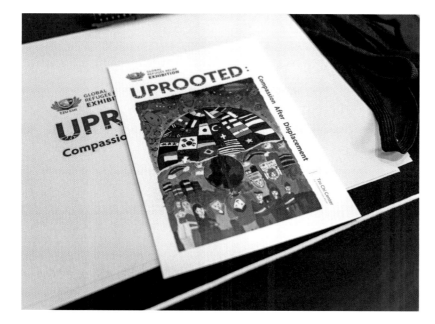

慈濟國際難民援助特展，2023

展覽明信片和宣傳資料。攝影：Héctor Muniente

個心碎的故事，有著對戰爭的恐懼，還有孩子們對慈濟的一份愛以及對於未來的希望，這些都淋漓盡致地展現在他們的畫作上。孩子們的畫作，從哀傷到希望，有層次感地展現，賦予整個展覽更深層的意境和無限的觸動。我們衷心期盼這個展覽，能帶來更多的啟發以及更多省思。

慈濟國際難民援助特展，2023

本次展覽的設計加入了反光材料的元素，觀眾在觀看展覽內容的同時，透過材料的反射性獲得了一個反觀自身的視角：難民們何以為家，而這也可能發生在我們任何一個人身上。攝影：羅奇華(上) / Philip Hwang(下)

慈濟國際難民援助特展，2023

展廳二樓的玻璃牆成為了本次展覽觀眾的留言牆，觀眾們紛紛留下對和平世界的祈願。這些美好的話語，如同蓮花花瓣一般，在留言牆上逐漸綻放。攝影：Philip Hwang (上) / 郭恩璞(下)

讓愛川流不息

貫穿人人的愛心，

讓愛川流不息，

為苦難人翻轉人生。

——證嚴上人靜思語

大愛

人文中心

Tzu Chi
Center

此心安住是吾家

沈慈知

慈濟大愛人文中心主任

慈濟大愛人文中心

上圖：慈濟大愛人文中心設立在離聯合國總部不遠的曼哈頓第60街，正面對面是一座歷史悠久的聖公會教堂(All Saints Episcopal Church)。攝影：范婷

右圖：慈濟大愛人文中心外觀。攝影：Philip Hwang

紐約曼哈頓第三大道往東轉入六十街後步行百米，矗立著一棟純白色五層樓高的小樓，與對街的聖公會教堂（All Saints Episcopal Church）和附近商鋪相比，它並沒有顯著的建築風格或標誌。當外牆上的旗幟，隨風忽悠地展開，慈濟標誌映入眼簾。它就是慈濟大愛人文中心 (Tzu Chi Center)，如此清新、簡潔的一棟小樓，每次走進去，上人對我的囑咐在耳畔迴響著：「這是慈濟比鄰聯合國的家，要好好照顧這個家。」

紐約曼哈頓是世界政治、經濟與文化的中心。在這繁忙的十字路口安置一個家，其所承載的責任與意義非凡。

該如何讓慈濟的價值觀通過這個家更廣泛地傳達出去，與紐約乃至全美不同背景、不同宗教的人群產生連結？懷抱著這個問題意識，作為佛教慈濟慈善基金會在全球範圍內的一個獨特場所，慈濟大愛人文中心的建立是為了實現以下目標：

一、作為慈濟面向世界的一扇窗口，讓世界了解、進而認同慈濟。

二、促進慈濟與世界各地有共同理念的夥伴關係，攜手支持人道主義倡議。

三、成為年輕一代慈濟人來參與、來體驗慈濟世界的平臺。

慈濟的理念與行動，皆源自佛陀的教誨，旨在啟發人性的善良，傳播愛的訊息，播撒長情與大愛的種籽，以建立溫馨祥和互助的社會。Tzu Chi Center 的中文名稱——「慈濟大愛人文

中心」也由此得來。

人們對「佛教組織」的想像，多半仍侷限於「通過自身修行來覺悟生命」，而少見將個體的修行積極投入到瞬息萬變的世界人群中去。慈濟自證嚴上人創建之初，就以社會使命為導向，跨越宗教的邊界、致力於人道主義救援，積極參與全人類共同面臨的問題。也正是如此，慈濟大愛人文中心象徵著慈濟安定社會的力量，也是傳達慈濟人文的場所。

二○一九年十月十三日，慈濟大愛人文中心正式揭幕，同時舉辦了《海地震後十年・讓希望延續》攝影展。在經歷了全球嚴酷的疫情之後，二○二二年九月，慈濟大愛人文中心舉辦長達一周的「全面應對氣候變遷峰會」。二○二三年六月，「根繫何處：流離失所後的慈悲共渡——慈濟國際難民援助特展」集中呈現了一九七九至二○二三年慈濟不間斷的國際難民援助的史蹟，同時也傳達了慈濟大愛人文中心對「此時、此地、此人」關懷與共情的佛學哲思。

三個樓層的布展內容中，第一樓層展示出深受戰火而流離中的敘利亞及烏克蘭人民接受全球慈濟的關懷與付出，以及我們救助塞爾維亞難民之紀錄，同時展示我們國際援助的歷史時間表。第二層樓展示出因內戰被迫流離失所的敘利亞孩子們在土耳其滿納海國際學校被全球慈濟人關懷後，他們因為「人間有愛」而自己繪圖抒發的心歷過程。第三層樓是「追隨佛陀」及「我思我師」，展示出慈濟基金會之緣起及回顧佛陀故鄉及佛陀

一生重要事跡。

展覽除了全球難民救援的圖像文獻外，其中一個動人的亮點——飛越數千英里、來自土耳其滿納海國際學校的難民孩子們質樸的繪畫，打動並撫慰了參觀者的心，也給予未來一個更直觀的使命。我想，這些孩子們畫作裡包含和傳達著對安定家園的渴望、對美與善的表達，這是世間永恆的真理，是我們心靈的根繫。

感恩你我有緣接觸慈濟世界，此際跟隨證嚴上人為全世界苦難眾生以真善美的大愛精神付出一點心力與關懷。「此心安住是吾家」。我們周遭世界永遠都面臨著許多挑戰，如同曼哈頓街頭無時不刻存在的喧鬧和警笛聲，而這棟小白樓，滿載著全球慈濟人堅定信念，讓社區的居民信賴，讓慈濟人感受到家的溫暖與力量。

我們盼望能為所有參訪的朋友播植一個善的種籽，讓慈濟大愛人文中心成為這粒種子生長啟蒙的家。在這裡，我們期盼消弭人與人的邊界與隔閡，讓大愛能無遠弗屆的傳播出去。

感恩大家的護持。

慈濟的理念與行動，皆源自佛陀的教誨，旨在啟發人性的善良，傳播愛的訊息，播撒長情與大愛的種籽，以建立溫馨祥和互助的社會。Tzu Chi Center 的中文名稱，「慈濟大愛人文中心」也由此得來。

慈濟大愛人文中心

上圖：慈濟人在大愛人文中心後院合影。攝影：Héctor Muniente

下圖：大愛人文中心外觀以及慈濟北美出版刊物。攝影：羅奇華

相知、相聚，於大愛

萬千慈濟人的身影，跨越地理、宗教的界限，積極地牽動起本地和國際的力量，共同交織成一個更完善持久的大愛網絡。無論是交流展示慈濟的人文項目或培育新的驅動力，大愛人文中心一直致力於傳達慈濟以愛與善念來推動世界進步的核心理念，也責無旁貸地成為了這一網絡中關鍵的連結點。

在「慈濟國際難民援助特展」舉辦期間，大愛人文中心籌辦了多項人文活動，並接待了數千人次的個人以及團體來參觀。緣起心中的「大愛」，我們相識相聚於「大愛」，並懷抱此念繼續前行。

相聚在慈濟大愛人文中心

上圖：2023年8月29日，精舍師父關懷團到訪大愛人文中心，參觀「慈濟國際難民援助特展」，眾人在門前合影。照片：慈濟大愛人文中心提供

下圖：2023年9月7日，慈濟基金會副執行長何日生赴美訪問期間，前來紐約到訪大愛人文中心，並參觀「慈濟國際難民援助特展」。攝影：劉音序

相聚在慈濟大愛人文中心

上圖：大愛人文中心參加「紐約開放日」(OHNY Weekend)活動，在2023年10月21-22日期間，民眾透過參觀「慈濟國際難民援助特展」、茶道、花道來認識和了解慈濟。攝影：劉輝

中圖：2023年10月25日，作家卡里瑪·羅曼尼夫(Karima Romaniv)攜帶她的出版書籍參觀展覽，分享了她在烏克蘭經歷戰爭和流離失所的故事、在波蘭與慈濟志工的因緣，以及在臺灣的新生活。照片：Karima Romaniv提供

下圖：2023年8月4日，慈濟布魯克林暑期營隊的學生參訪人文中心，透過導覽學習慈濟志工如何以感恩、尊重、愛來提供救援服務。大愛人文中心主任沈慈知為學生們講解。照片：慈濟大愛人文中心提供

泰國清邁府訪視關懷，1994

泰北三年扶困計畫；靜思精舍德旻師父關懷難民村的小朋友。攝影：黃錦益

2014.10

Food, supplies, heating fuel, and living allowances for Syrian refugee families in Istanbul, Türkiye.

為土耳其伊斯坦堡的敘利亞難民家庭提供食物、物資、暖氣燃料和生活津貼。

2015.01

Establishment of El Menahil International School for Syrian refugee children in Istanbul, Türkiye.

在土耳其伊斯坦堡為敘利亞難民兒童建立滿納海國際學校。

2015.01

Tzu Chi Thailand and U.S. Department of State agreement to provide medical aid for refugees in Bangkok.

慈濟泰國分會與美國國務院達成協議，為曼谷境內難民提供醫療援助。

2016.03

Aid operation providing winter clothes and hot food for Syrians staying in refugee camps in Serbia.

為居住在塞爾維亞難民營的敘利亞人提供冬衣和熱食等援助。

2016.03

Medical expenses for Syrian children in Jordan's Za'atari Refugee Camp through AMR (American Medical Response) clinics.

通過約旦扎阿塔里難民營的AMR診所，為敘利亞兒童提供醫療費用援助。

2016.03

Set up of the first clinic in Türkiye to provide medical services for Syrian refugees.

在土耳其設立第一家義診中心，為敘利亞難民提供醫療服務。

2017.02

Clothing and daily food for families sheltered in the Obrenovac Refugee Camp in Serbia.

為塞爾維亞歐普難民中心的家庭提供衣物和日常食物。

2022.04

Immediate financial aid leading to long-term assistance for Ukrainian refugees in Poland and other countries.

為波蘭和其他國家的烏克蘭難民提供急難經濟援助，後發展為長期援助。

2022.05

Purchase of land to build a permanent El Menahil International School campus in Istanbul, Türkiye.

在土耳其伊斯坦堡購買土地，作為建造滿納海國際學校的永久校址。

2022

Tzu Chi Refugee Relief Timeline
慈濟難民援助大事記

1979

1979.02
Emergency assistance for Vietnamese refugees resettling in the Penghu Islands in the Taiwan Strait.
緊急援助安置在臺灣海峽澎湖列島的越南難民。

1994.07
Medical and food aid for refugees from Rwanda in collaboration with Médecins du Monde, France.
與法國「世界醫師聯盟」合作，為盧安達難民提供醫療和糧食援助。

1995.01
A multi-faceted aid program for refugees in Thailand, help that continues till this day.
對泰國境內的難民提供多方位援助計畫，一直持續至今。

1995.10
Emergency medical assistance for refugees from Chechnya in collaboration with Médecins du Monde, France. 與法國「世界醫師聯盟」合作，為車臣難民提供緊急醫療援助。

1998.01
Supplies for families in the Baqa'a, Jerash, and Aqaba refugee camps for Palestinians in Jordan.
為約旦境內巴卡阿、傑拉什和阿卡巴難民營的巴勒斯坦家庭提供物資援助。

2001.11
Supplies for refugees in Afghanistan along the border, in collaboration with US-based Knightsbridge International.
與美國「國際騎士橋救援組織」合作，為阿富汗邊境地區的難民提供物資。

2005.03
Memorandum of Understanding between Tzu Chi Malaysia and the United Nations High Commissioner for Refugees (UNHCR) to provide aid in detention camps.
慈濟馬來西亞分會與聯合國難民署簽定合作備忘錄，為扣留營的難民提供援助。

2009.01
Emergency funds and other supplies for patients from Gaza in Jordan's Queen Alia Military Hospital.
為約旦阿麗亞王后軍事醫院中來自加薩的病患提供緊急資金和其他物資支援。

2011.12
Food distributions as vital assistance for Syrian refugees in Mafraq Province, Jordan.
為約旦馬弗拉克省的敘利亞難民糧食發放提供重要援助。

播種才能萌芽

從小教育孩子發揮愛心，
種下粒粒善的種子，
善念就會萌芽成長。

——證嚴上人靜思語

來自

滿納海

的色彩

Colors

from

El Menahil

從沙漠走向綠洲──一封來自滿納海校長的信

主麻教授（Cuma Serya）

敘利亞西北部戰爭期間，一名境內流離失所的女孩坐在一輛毀壞的車輛裡。雖然戰爭帶來的是支離破碎的家園，但孩子臉上露出的溫暖微笑裡仍蘊藏著對未來的希望。照片：土耳其「世界醫師聯盟」提供

那名孩子的哭聲仍然在我的耳邊迴蕩，當他試圖掙脫母親的手，想跟隨他的哥哥去上學時，他問說：為什麼我不能去呢？

母親的回答充滿痛苦：明年就輪到你上學，然後哥哥去工廠，你們輪換。

這就是敘利亞人在逃難至土耳其的過程中所經歷的情景，你能看到有些敘利亞難民孩子站在家的陽臺上，朝著背著書包上學去的土耳其孩子揮手；還有一些孩子站在家門口，一直看著直到校車離去，回憶著曾在敘利亞的學校門前嬉戲和學習的日子。

此刻，孩子的母親站在後面，輕撫著孩子的頭，含淚安慰說：有一天你也會去學校的，我的孩子。

教育能夠提升一個民族，反之，缺乏教育則會使民族陷入困境。在土耳其，整整一個世代的敘利亞兒童正身陷無知和文盲的境地之中。

二〇一四年末，與胡光中先生的會面給我們帶來了一線希望。在解釋了孩子們如果繼續失學將在未來面臨的風險後，胡光中先生親自擔起了這個項目的重任，並特地為此前往臺灣。經過了長時間的討論和審議，一開始有少數學生獲得了資助批准，然後我們開始與蘇丹加濟（Sultan Ghazi）地區的教育局進行會議和討論，提出了為敘利亞難民兒童建立一所學校的想法。最終，慈濟獲准在尼吉布‧法德爾（Najib Fadel）學校創辦了滿納海國際學校的第一所分校。

二〇一五年一月二十三日一早，我們來到了尼吉布‧法德爾學校，這個日期也將永遠被敘利亞人記住。在這所由約五百七十名學生開始的學校裡，你無法想像學生們第一天上學的反應、感動以及激動的情緒。那是語言無法形容的時刻，令人永生難忘。

滿納海這項專案就如同一場降臨在貧瘠土地的雨，為這片土地創造了一個百花齊放而充滿生機的綠洲，花兒會讓這片未來的家園充滿芬芳。

到第二年的時候，我們已經擁有了三所學校，學生人數超過二千四百名。由於取得的成功，到了第三年，我們共建立了七所分校，學生人數多達到三千二百名。後來，滿納海成為了土耳其各地學校的典範。

然而，所有這些喜悅背後的痛苦並沒有結束，許多學生因為要養家仍然無法上學。我們必須尋找解決方案，使他們能夠重返學校。事實上，我們在這些學生和他們的家庭中遇到了一個很大的問題，那就是該如何讓這些學生回到學校，又不損害他們家庭的生計呢？最終，慈濟決定為每位學生提供每月的家庭補助金，補助的金額與他們之前打工能獲得的薪水相同。

二〇一七年，我們開辦了一所完全免費的國際學校，讓學生在那裡學習知識和道德，這所學校現在容納了約四千五百名學生，包括正式教育課程、週末課程以及土耳其和英語語言課程。

如果我們來談談那些在進入了滿納海國際學校後生活發生了巨大變化的學生們，那麼雪曼（Shaimaa）就是一個例子，她在還是個嬰兒的時候就失去了父親。來到土耳其之後雪曼被迫在工廠工作，她也失去了實現夢想的機會。多虧了滿納海國際學校以及她在學校裡獲得的獎學金，她現在已是伊斯坦堡的一所頂尖大學的學生。另一個例子是學生法赫里‧謝赫‧拉希德（Fakhri Al-Sheikh Rashid），他輟學多年，靠在工廠打工以獲取微薄的薪水。但在入學滿納海並獲得獎學金和精神支持後，他考得了全年級最高分，現在已經是醫學院的二年級學生。

這就是滿納海國際學校，它已經改變了整整一代人，將他們的生活從絕望轉變為希望。數百名學生由此得以進入土耳其的學院和大學，獲得知識與品德。

來自滿納海的色彩

123

土耳其滿納海國際學校｜**El Menahil International School**
與學生們在一起的主麻教授｜Cuma Serya with students
攝影｜Photo: Jaime Puerta